ScottForesman Science

Discover the Wonder

Series Consulting Author

David Heil
Associate Director,
Oregon Museum of Science & Industry
Portland, Oregon

Consulting Authors

Maureen Allen
Science Resource Teacher/Specialist
Irvine Unified School District
Irvine, California

Dr. Timothy Cooney
Professor of Earth Science & Science Education
Earth Science Department
University of Northern Iowa
Cedar Falls, Iowa

Dr. Angie L. Matamoros
Science Curriculum Specialist K–12
Broward County Schools
Ft. Lauderdale, Florida

Dr. Manuel Perry
Manager, Educational Programs
Lawrence Livermore National Laboratory
Livermore, California

Dr. Irwin Slesnick
Professor of Biology
Biology Department
Western Washington University
Bellingham, Washington

ScottForesman

A Division of HarperCollinsPublishers

Editorial Offices: Glenview, Illinois
Regional Offices: Sunnyvale, California • Tucker, Georgia
Glenview, Illinois • Oakland, New Jersey • Dallas, Texas

Content Consultants

Dr. Linda Berne
Department of Health Promotion
and Kinesiology
University of North Carolina
Charlotte, North Carolina

Dr. Bonnie J. Buratti
Jet Propulsion Laboratory
California Institute of Technology
Pasadena, California

Dr. Norman M. Gelfand
Physicist
Fermi National Accelerator Laboratory
Accelerator Division
Batavia, Illinois

Dr. Roger A. Pielke
Professor
Department of Atmospheric Science
Colorado State University
Fort Collins, Colorado

Dr. Harrison H. Schmitt
*Former Astronaut (Apollo 17) and
United States Senator
Geologist and Science and
Technology Consultant*
Albuquerque, New Mexico

Dr. Lisa K. Wagner
Department of Biology
Georgia Southern University
Statesboro, Georgia

Multicultural Consultants

Dr. Frank Dukepoo
Department of Biology
Northern Arizona University
Flagstaff, Arizona

Dr. Amram Gamiel
*Educational Consultant
Professional Writer*
Newton Center, Massachusetts

Dr. Anthony R. Sancho
*Director of Hispanic Health
Education Center*
Southwest Regional Laboratory
Los Alamitos, California

Dr. Deborah A. Fortune
Department of Health Promotion
and Kinesiology
University of North Carolina
Charlotte, North Carolina

Dr. Luis A. Martinez-Perez
College of Education
Florida International University
Miami, Florida

Math/Science Consultant

Catherine R. Ney
Teacher
Blacksburg, Virginia
1994–95 Christa McAuliffe Fellow,
State of Virginia

Acknowledgments

Photographs Unless otherwise acknowledged, all photographs are the property of Scottforesman. Page abbreviations are as follows: (T)top, (C)center, (B)bottom, (L)left, (R)right, (INS)inset.

Cover Design Sheldon Cotler + Associates

Cover Background: Willard Clay Photography inset: L. West/P.G.
Magnifying Glass: Richard Chesnut

Page iv(T) John Shaw/Bruce Coleman, Inc. **vii** Luann Benoit
viii(T) E. R. Degginger **ix** W. Hill/The Image Works **x** John Cancalosi/Peter Arnold, Inc. **x(T)** David Scharf/Peter Arnold, Inc. **xii(T)** CoCoMcCoy/Rainbow **xiii(T)** Barry Parker/Bruce Coleman, Inc. **xiii(B)** T. Savino/The Image Works **xiv** Garv Griffen/Animals **xv** Stephen J. Krasemann/DRK Photo

Illustrations Unless otherwise acknowledged, all computer graphics by The Quarasan Group, Inc. **Page v** Ebet Dudley **ix** Jan Palmer

Acknowledgments continue on page 47.

About the Cover

This striking monarch butterfly was photographed in its Michigan habitat. Monarchs, though, are a common sight across the continental United States. They live in habitats such as that shown in the background photograph— a field of mule-ears near Washington Pass in Gunnison National Forest in Colorado.

Safety Consultant

Dr. Jack A. Gerlovich
*Science Education Safety
Consultant/Author*
Drake University
Des Moines, Iowa

Reading Consultants

Dr. Joan Develin Coley
*Director of Graduate Reading
Program*
Western Maryland College
Westminster, Maryland

Dr. Robert A. Pavlik
*Professor of Reading/
Language Arts*
Reading/Language Arts
Department
Cardinal Stritch College
Milwaukee, Wisconsin

Activity Consultant

Mary Jo Diem
Science/Educational Consultant
Croton-on-Hudson, New York

Reviewers

Mary Anne Brown
Science Specialist
St. Pius X Elementary School
Mission, Kansas

Dr. Robert L. Christopher
Supervisor of Elementary Schools
Harford County Public Schools
Bel Air, Maryland

Sharon A. Craig
Reading Specialist
Friendship Valley Elementary
School
Westminster, Maryland

Norma J. Doolittle
Teacher
Thomas Watson Elementary School
Endicott, New York

Dr. Deborah J. Dyer
*Director of Research and
Evaluation*
Portsmouth Public Schools
Portsmouth, Virginia

Kim L. Fleming
Teacher
Clark Elementary School
Paducah, Kentucky

Carol Gilberty-Rimondi
Teacher
Maria Colon Sanchez School
Hartford, Connecticut

JoCasta Green
Teacher
Madison School
Madison, Alabama

Marie L. Harris
Teacher
Ralph Downs Elementary School
Putnam City Schools
Oklahoma City, Oklahoma

Kathy Jeranek
Teacher
Lake Wylie School
Charlotte, North Carolina

Linda Kane
Teacher
Palm Lake Elementary School
Orlando, Florida

Kathleen K. Liska
Teacher
Mill Street School
Naperville, Illinois

Diane L. Lucas
Teacher
Hartwood Elementary School
Pittsburgh, Pennsylvania

Dr. Charles William McLaughlin
Coordinator of Science Education
St. Joseph Public Schools
St. Joseph, Missouri

Julia S. McLeod
Teacher
Brennen Elementary School
Columbia, South Carolina

Henrietta Pane
Teacher
Westgate Elementary School
Omaha, Nebraska

Melinda A. Rials
Teacher
John Love Elementary School
Jacksonville, Florida

Pat J. Roller
*Facilitator for Science Resource
Center*
Tulsa Public School System
Tulsa, Oklahoma

Kathy Sabella
Early Childhood Specialist
New Hanover County School
District
Wilmington, North Carolina

Darla G. Simms
Teacher
J.R. Ewan Elementary School
Lexington, Kentucky

Donna Witt
Teacher
Palm Lake Elementary School
Orlando, Florida

Module A

Plants

Chapter 2

Looking at Plants A 22

Lesson 1
How are plants alike?
Discover Activity
A 23

Lesson 2
What are the parts of a plant? Visual/Verbal
A 24

Lesson 3
How do leaves help plants?
A 26

Lesson 4
How do roots help plants?
A 28

Lesson 5
How do stems help plants?
A 30

Lesson 6
How do seeds grow into plants?
A 32

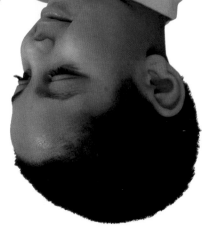

Growing and Changing

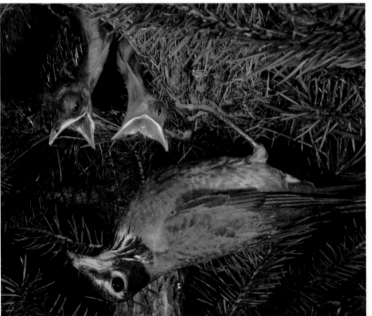

Chapter 2

How Animals Grow B 24

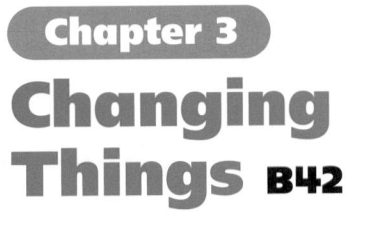

Chapter 3
Changing Things B42

Sound and Light

Module C

Sound and Light

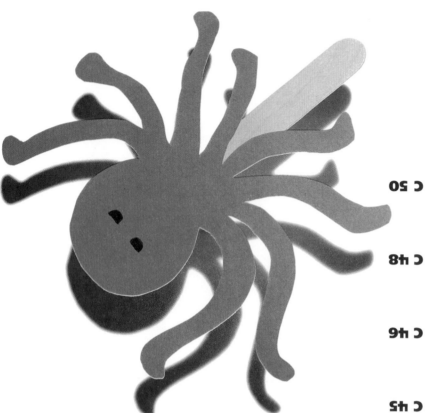

Chapter 3

Light C 44

Weather

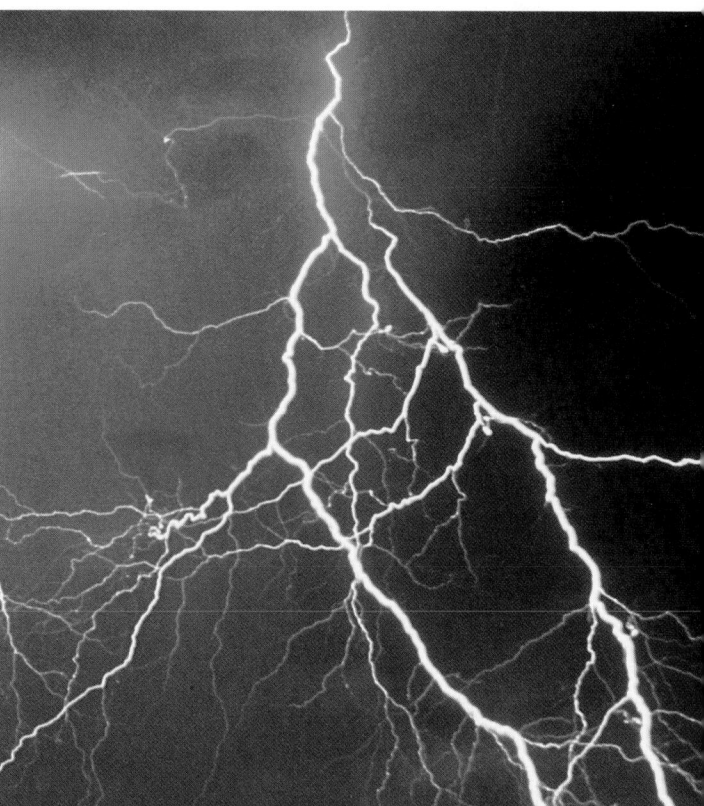

Chapter 2

Air, Water, and Weather D 22

Module A

Plants

Plants

How are trees, carrots, and dandelions alike?
They are all plants! Plants grow in forests
and along city streets. They even grow in
sidewalk cracks.

Chapter 1

Looking at Trees

Think about an apple seed.
How can a big tree grow
from something so small?
Page **A 4**

Chapter 2
Looking at Plants
Plants do not eat like you do. Where do plants get what they need to grow? Page **A 22**

Chapter 3
How Plants Are Used
Could you live in a tree? If you could, you would have to share your home.
Page A 44

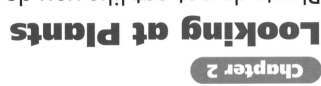

Chapter 1

Looking at Trees

Do all the children in your class look alike? How do you tell one another apart? Hair color, size, or shape might help you. Getting to know your classmates can be fun.

Getting to know trees is also fun. Think about the kinds of trees in the world. How can you tell them apart?

What is a tree?

1. Think about different trees you see.
2. Draw a picture of your favorite tree.
3. Share your tree picture with your class.
4. **Tell about it.** Tell about your tree. What makes it different from other trees? How is it like other trees?

Ask me what else I want to find out about trees.

How are trees alike?

Trees may look different. But trees are alike in some ways. Trees have the same parts. Find the parts of a tree in the picture.

The **trunk** is the part that holds the tree up. Find the branches. A **branch** is a part that grows from the trunk. Now, move your finger along a branch to the leaves. Most trees have some kind of leaf.

trunk

Trees have another part that you may not see. Most roots of trees grow under the ground. The roots hold the tree in the ground. Find the roots of this tree.

branches

leaves

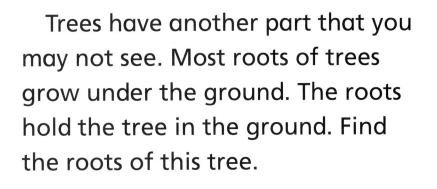

Checkpoint

Make a model of a tree. What parts does a tree have?

roots

What are some kinds of trees?

Look at the different kinds of trees. Which of these trees grow near where you live?

Different kinds of trees grow in different places. Look at the palm tree. Where does this tree grow? What other trees grow in warm places? Where do maple trees grow? Maple trees also grow in forests and in cities.

Checkpoint

Choose one tree from the pictures. Tell how it is different from the other trees.

Palm trees grow in warm places.

Nut pine trees grow in warm, dry places.

Willow trees grow in warm and cold places.

Pine trees grow in warm places and in cold places.

Maple trees grow well in fields and on farms.

What shapes can trees have?

circle

triangle

oval

You found out that trees have the same parts. You also found out that different kinds of trees grow in different places. But trees are different in another way too.

Look at the trees in the pictures. Each of these trees has a different shape. Find the tree that has the shape of a circle. What other shapes do you see?

Find the shape of a tree.

You will need: crayons shapes from your teacher

1. Choose a shape.
2. Look at the trees on page 8 and page 9.
   Find a tree that matches the shape.
3. Draw the tree inside the shape. Write the name of the tree.

Checkpoint

Tell the shape of the tree. What other shapes do trees have?

How can you group leaves?

You looked at different kinds of trees. You saw that trees have different shapes. The leaves of trees are also different. You can find out how leaves are different.

You will need:

 10 different leaves

crayons

yarn

Find out about it.

1 Work with a team.

2 Look at the sizes, shapes, and colors of the leaves. How are the leaves alike? How are they different?

3 Talk about how many kinds of leaves you have. Make a yarn circle for each kind. Sort the leaves into groups.

Write about it.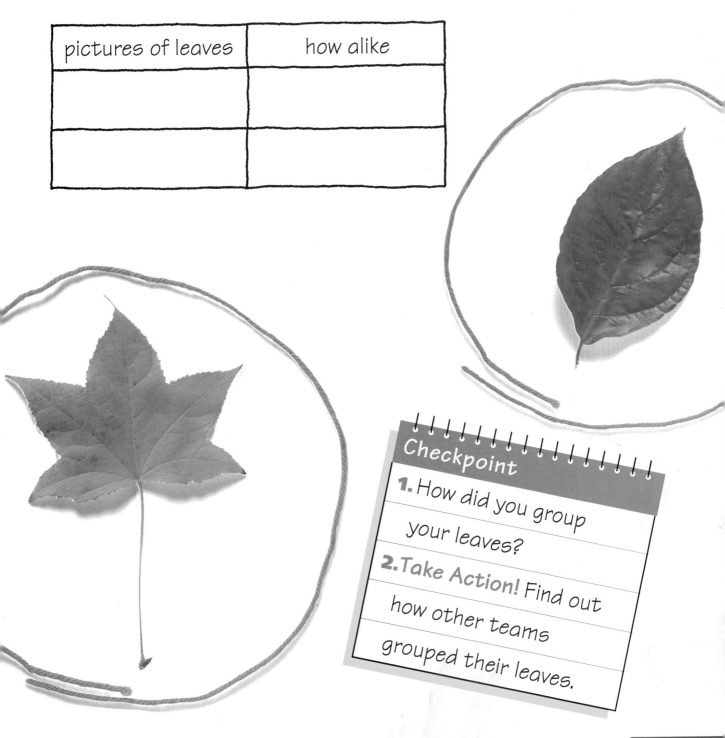

Make a chart like this one. Draw or trace each leaf on the chart. Put leaves that are in the same group together.

pictures of leaves	how alike

Checkpoint

1. How did you group your leaves?
2. Take Action! Find out how other teams grouped their leaves.

What are other kinds of leaves?

The leaves you grouped are called **broad leaves.** Most trees with broad leaves lose all of their leaves each fall. They grow new leaves each spring.

Look at the leaves in the pictures. How are these leaves different from the ones you grouped? What shapes are these leaves?

These leaves are called **needles.** Trees with needles don't lose all their leaves in the fall. They lose some needles at different times in the year. New needles grow. And trees with needles stay green all the time.

Needles are like other leaves in some ways. Needles have different sizes and shapes. How many different needles can you find?

Checkpoint

Tell how broad leaves and needles are different.

What do tree seeds do?

Tree seeds have different sizes and shapes. Some tree seeds, like the seeds in the pictures, are inside coverings. But all tree seeds are alike in one way. All tree seeds can grow into new trees.

Plant a tree seed.

You will need: tree seeds   soil   plastic cup   water

1. Fill a cup with soil.
2. Plant the tree seed your teacher gives you in the soil. Water the soil.
3. Put the cup in a warm, sunny place.
4. Add a few drops of water to the soil each day.

Checkpoint

Draw pictures of what you see. How are the seeds alike?

How old is your tree?

The trunk of a tree gets bigger around as the tree grows. Some trees grow about the same amount each year. You can find out about how old these trees are by measuring their trunks.

1. Look at the two trees in the drawing. The trunk of tree A measures 30 centimeters around. Centimeters are marked cm. How big is the trunk of tree B?

tree A
30 cm

2. The chart helps you find out the age of a tree. Tree A is 30 centimeters around. Find 30 centimeters in the chart. A tree that is 30 centimeters around is about 12 years old.

size of tree trunk	age of tree
20 cm	about 8 years
25 cm	about 10 years
30 cm	about 12 years

tree B
20 cm

Checkpoint

1. About how old is a tree that is 20 centimeters around?

2. How old is tree B?

What did you learn?

Now you know how trees are alike. Make a puzzle to show what you have learned.

You will need:  construction paper   crayons
    scissors

Make a tree puzzle.

1. Draw a picture of a tree. Show all the parts of the tree.
2. Cut your picture into 10 puzzle pieces.
3. Mix up your puzzle pieces.
4. Trade puzzles with a classmate.
5. Put the puzzle together.

Share what you learned.

1. What parts of a tree did you draw?
2. How are trees alike?
3. What is your favorite tree? Why?

Chapter 2

Looking at Plants

Pretend you are a famous plant detective. You can find plants no matter where they are growing! You even find them in sidewalk cracks.

Suppose you are looking for plants in your neighborhood. What kind of plants will you find? How are all these plants alike?

How are plants alike?

1. Find a picture of a tree.
2. List words that tell about the tree.
3. Look at a plant in your classroom. List words that tell about the plant.
4. **Tell about it.** Find the words on your lists that are the same.

Ask me what else I want to find out about plants.

What are the parts of a plant?

When you look at a tree, what do you see? You probably see the leaves and the trunk. You might know that a tree trunk is a stem.

Stems are parts of many plants. Find the stems in the pictures. What other plant parts can you find in the pictures?

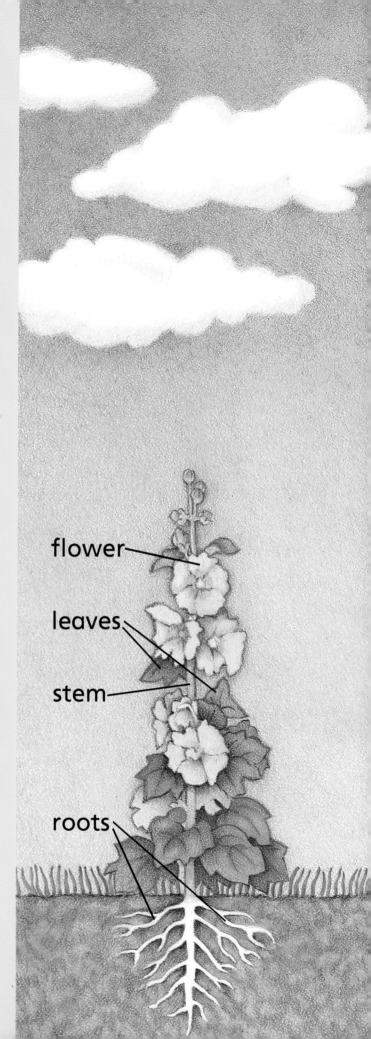

flower

leaves

stem

roots

Checkpoint

Use paper or clay to make a model of a plant.

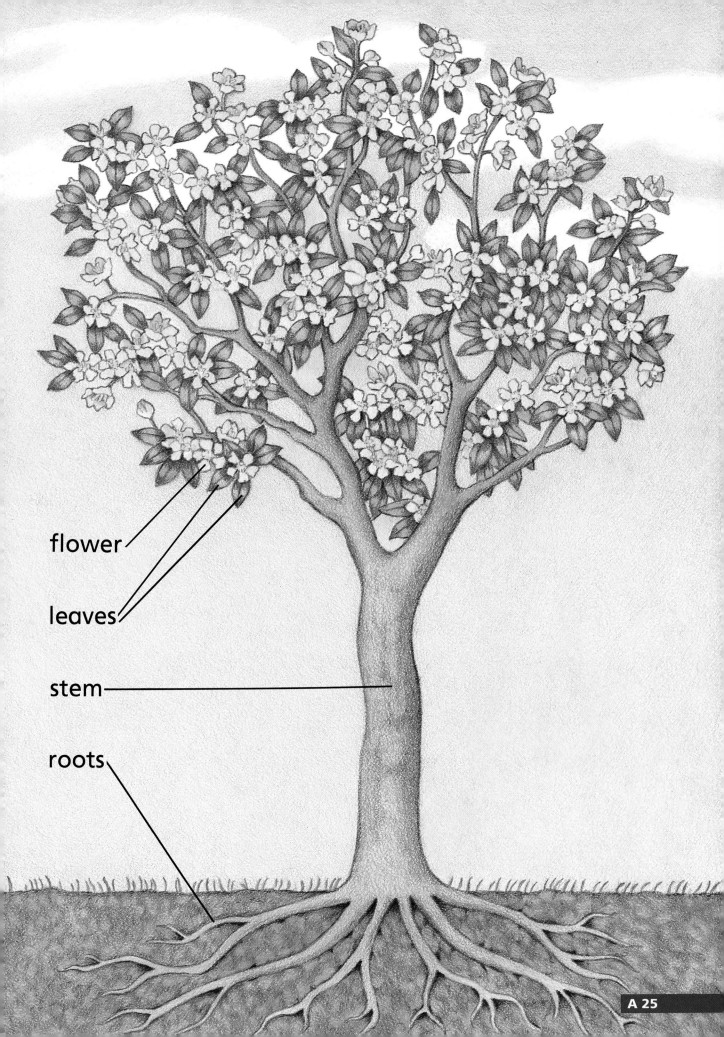

flower

leaves

stem

roots

How do leaves help plants?

Have you ever seen a tree eat? Of course not! Trees and other plants do not eat the way you do. You need to eat food to help you grow. Plants need food to help them grow too. Plants make their own food.

The **leaves** of a plant make the food that plants need. Leaves use sunlight, air, and water to make food. Can a plant live without leaves? Let's find out.

Remove the leaves.

You will need:  2 plants 🥛 water ✂ scissors

1. Put 2 plants near a sunny window.
2. Cut the leaves off 1 plant. Cut off any new leaves that grow on it.
3. Water both plants.

Checkpoint

Make a chart that tells what happens to the plants. Why does a plant need leaves?

How do roots help plants?

A strong wind is blowing. Why don't plants blow away? If you could look under the soil, you would see why!

See how deep into the soil these **roots** grow. How do roots keep plants from blowing away? Roots help plants in another way too. They take in water from the soil.

grass   carrot   dandelion

Observe roots.

You will need: 🪴 plant ⬜ plastic jar 〰️ foil ☕ water ✏️ crayon

1. Fill a jar about half full of water.
2. Put a plant in the jar. The roots must be in the water.
3. Cover the top of the jar with foil.
4. Mark the top of the water in the jar. Use a crayon.
5. Look at the jar each day. What happens to the water?

Checkpoint

Tell what happened to the water in the jar. Why did this happen?

How do stems help plants?

You know that roots take in water from the soil. You also know that leaves use water to make food. The water has to get from the roots to the leaves.

Roots and **stems** have tubes inside of them. The tubes carry water from the roots to the leaves and flowers.

Watch water move in a plant.

You will need:  food coloring   white flower

plastic cup   water

1. Fill a plastic cup half full with water.
2. Add 6 drops of food coloring.
3. Put the flower in the cup. What do you think will happen?
4. Watch the flower for 2 days.

Checkpoint

Tell about what happened to the flower. How did the colored water get to the flower?

How do seeds grow into plants?

Suppose you look inside a bean **seed.** You can see different parts. How many parts can you find in the picture? What are the names of the parts?

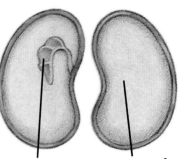

baby plant   stored food

Find out how this seed grows into a bean plant. Look at the picture of the growing seed. What part begins to grow first? Now watch how a seed grows into a bean plant.

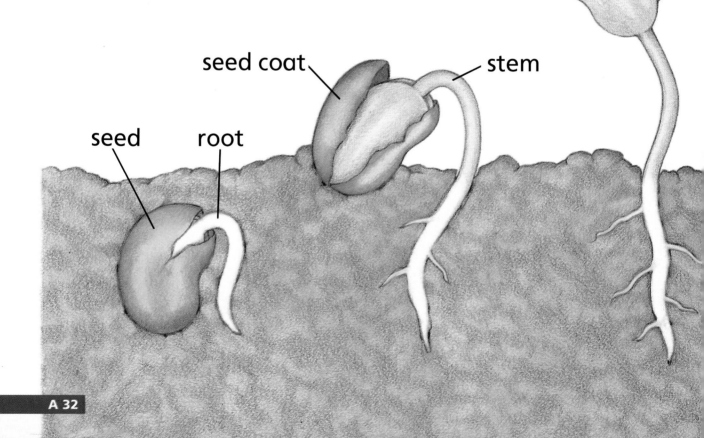

leaves

seed coat   stem

seed   root

Watch a seed grow.

You will need:  soaked bean seeds ⬜ plastic bag

🧻 paper towel 🥤 water

1. Look at a seed. What parts do you see?
2. Take the seed apart. Find the baby plant. Where is the stored food?
3. Put a wet paper towel inside a plastic bag.
4. Put 4 bean seeds on top of the wet paper towel. Close the bag.
5. Watch the seeds for a few days.

Checkpoint

Write about how bean seeds grow into plants.

What do seeds need to grow?

You saw that bean seeds need water to grow. What else do you think seeds need to start growing?

You will need:

2 cups

cotton

16 seeds

water

plastic wrap

crayon

masking tape

Find out about it.

1 Fill 2 cups with cotton.

2 Pour some water into each cup.

3 Put 8 seeds on top of the cotton in each cup.

4 Cover each of the cups with plastic wrap.

5 Write *warm* on 1 cup. Put that cup in a warm place.

6 Write *cold* on the other cup. Put that cup in a refrigerator.

7 Look at the seeds each day.

Write about it.

Make a chart like this one. Write or draw what the seeds look like.

day	warm place	cold place
1		
2		
3		

Checkpoint

1. In which place did the seeds grow better?
2. Take Action! Draw a picture to show what time of the year you would plant seeds.

warm

Cold

What do plants need to grow?

Pretend this garden is yours. How can you make sure your plants grow? Think about what plants need.

Remember that plants need sunlight, air, and water. Plants use these things to make food. So, pick a sunny spot for your garden. Make sure your plants get air and water. Where will your plants get air? How will they get water?

BEETS

LETTUCE

Your plants need other things too. The plants in the picture grow best where it is warm. So, start your garden when the weather is warm.

You know that most plants need soil to grow in. They also need plenty of space. Be sure your plants are far enough apart.

Checkpoint

Pretend you are a plant.
Tell what you need to grow.

SPINACH

BEANS

RADISHES

How are soils different?

    You found out that plants need soil. Where have you seen soil? What was the soil like? Maybe it was hard or soft. The color of soil can be dark or light. It can be brown or red.

    Look at the different kinds of soil. You can see that soil is made of different things. Find out what is in your soil.

Shake your soil.

You will need:  plastic jar with lid   water   soil

1. Put some soil in the jar.
2. Fill the jar with water.
3. Cover the jar with the lid.
4. Shake the jar 15 times.
5. Wait a few minutes.
6. Look at the soil. What do you see?

Checkpoint

Tell what things you see in the jar. What kind of soil do you see?

What soil is best for some plants?

You saw three different kinds of soil—sand, clay, and loam. You can find out which soil is best for some plants. How? You can measure how tall plants grow in different soils.

1. Look at the plant in sand. It is 2 centimeters tall.
2. How tall is the plant growing in the clay?
3. How tall is the plant in the loam?

4. Draw a chart like this one.

5. Color your chart to show how tall the plant in the loam is.

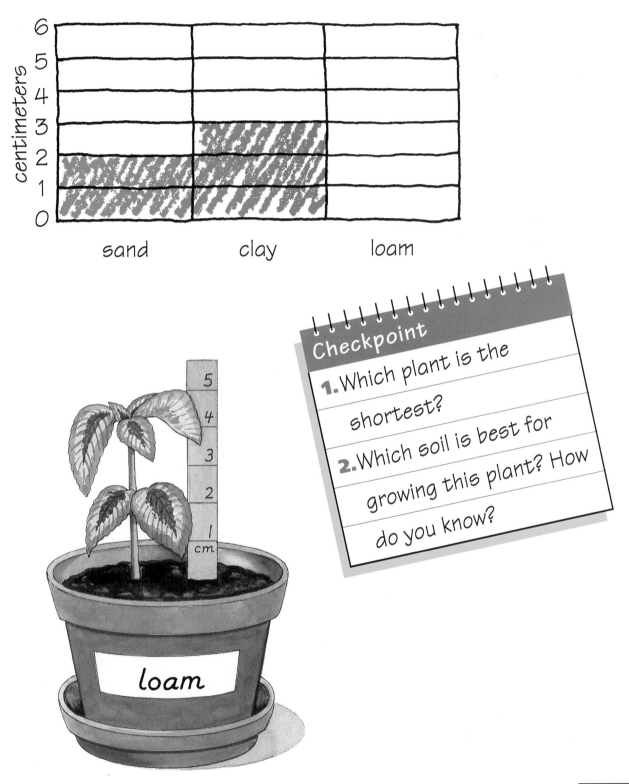

Checkpoint

1. Which plant is the shortest?

2. Which soil is best for growing this plant? How do you know?

What did you learn?

You can buy seeds for plants in a store. They come in a small package. A seed package tells about the plants that will grow from the seeds. It also tells what the plant needs to grow. Imagine a plant you would like to grow. How can you make a seed package for that plant?

You will need: big envelope   crayons or markers
paper   scissors

Make a seed package.

1. Draw your imaginary plant on the front of a big envelope. Show all the plant parts.
2. Write a name for your plant.
3. Turn the envelope over. Write how long it takes for the plants to grow. Write where the plants will grow best.
4. Draw some seeds for your plant. Put them in your seed package.

Share what you learned.

1. Where would be a good place to grow your plant? Why?
2. What parts does your plant have?

Chapter 3

How Plants Are Used

Do you like to look for things? You can do it in your classroom. Look around. Find things that come from plants.

You are already looking in a good place. This book comes from a plant. What kind of a plant do you think it comes from? Let's find out what other things come from plants.

Which things come from plants?

1. Look at each object. Feel it. Tell what it is.
2. Group the objects that come from plants.
3. Group the objects that do not come from plants.
4. **Tell about it.** Tell why you put each object in its group.

Ask me what else I want to find out about how plants are used.

My First Picture Dictionary

POCKET MEMO

How do people use plants?

People use plants for food. Think about what you ate yesterday. Do you think you ate food from a plant? If you ate an apple, you were eating food from a plant.

People use plants for clothes. Some of your clothes may be made of cotton. Look at the cotton. Cotton comes from a plant. What cotton clothes can you find in the picture?

cotton plant

People use wood from plants. What things in your classroom are made from wood? What toys do you have that are made of wood? Is your home made from wood?

Checkpoint

Draw pictures of things you get from plants.

What parts of plants do you eat?

Look at the foods on this page. All of these foods are parts of plants. Which of these foods do you eat?

When you eat a carrot you are eating a root! What other roots do you eat? Let's find out what other plant parts you eat.

leaves

roots

stem

seeds

Group the foods.

You will need:  pictures of foods   crayons

4 paper plates

1. Write the word *leaves* on one paper plate.
2. Do the same thing for *roots,* for *stems,* and for *seeds.*
3. Decide which picture belongs on each plate. Put the pictures on the plates.

leaves

stems

roots

seeds

Checkpoint

Tell which parts of plants you eat.

What parts of plants do birds eat?

Like you, many animals get food from plants. Many animals, such as birds, eat plant seeds. What kinds of birds eat seeds? How can you find out?

You will need:

pine cone

peanut butter

birdseed

string

plastic knife

Find out about it.

1 Tie a piece of string to a pine cone.

2 Spread peanut butter on the pine cone.

3 Roll the pine cone in birdseed.

4 Hang the pine cone outside.

5 Watch the birds that eat the birdseed.

Write about it.

Make a chart like this one. Write what birds you saw at your bird feeder. Or you may draw a picture of the birds.

birds I saw

Checkpoint

1. What kind of bird did you see most often?

2. What part of a plant did the birds eat?

3. Take Action! Use a book to find the names of the birds.

What animals live in trees?

You know that plants are food for animals. But have you thought of a tree as a home for animals?

Look at the picture. What animals are living in these trees? Did any of the animals surprise you?

Animals live in all parts of a tree. Many animals even live under the bark. In what part of the tree does each animal live?

Checkpoint

Pretend you are a tree.
Let animals know what
places you have where
they can live.

caterpillar

beetle

squirrel

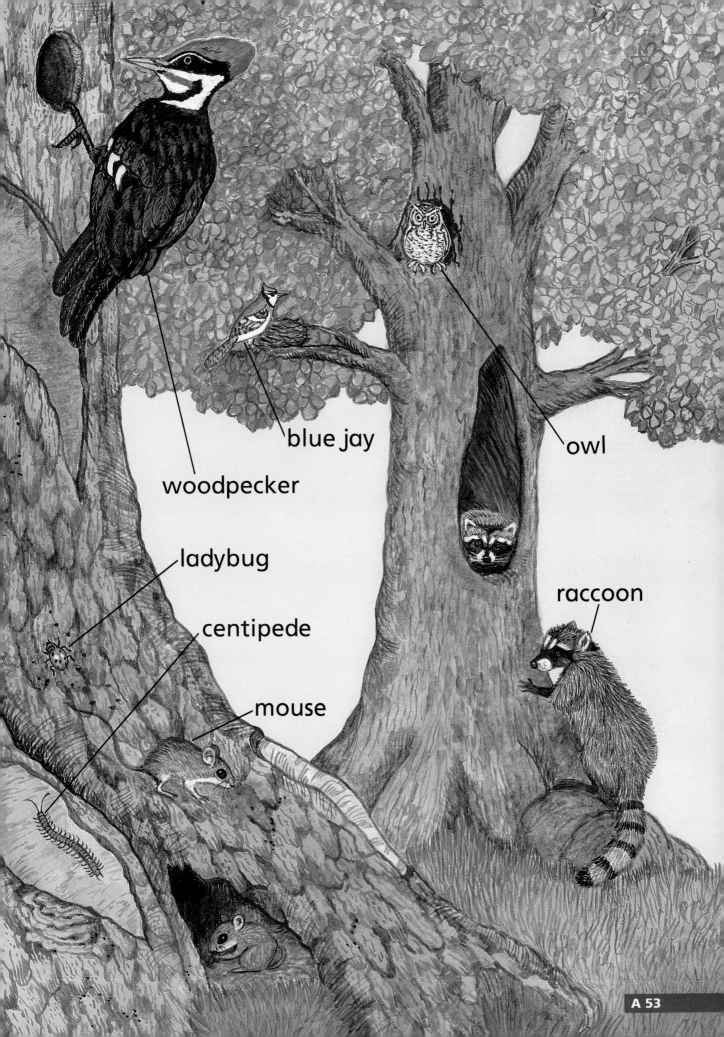

blue jay

owl

woodpecker

raccoon

ladybug

centipede

mouse

Where would you plant a tree?

Have you ever stood under a big tree on a hot, sunny day? It's much cooler than standing in the sun. Trees can even help keep your home cool.

Why do you think the cows are lying under a tree? Animals look for shade on hot days too.

You might think trees are very helpful.
Would you like to plant a tree? Where would
you want to plant it?

Checkpoint

Draw a place you would like to see a tree growing.
Draw a tree in your picture. Tell why you would like to plant the tree.

How do people use trees?

Many trees are cut down. The wood is used in three ways. The first way to use wood is to make lumber. The second way to use wood is to make paper. The third way to use wood is to burn it. Burning wood makes heat. The heat can be used to warm a house.

1. Look at the picture of the ten trees. Five trees are used for lumber.
2. How many trees are used to make paper?
3. How many trees are used for heat?

lumber

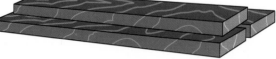

4. Draw a chart like this one.

5. Write the number of trees used for paper.

6. Write the number of trees used for heat.

use of trees	number of trees used
lumber	5
paper	
heat	

Checkpoint

1. Tell what most trees that are cut down are used for.

2. In which way do you use trees most?

paper

heat

What did you learn?

What are the ways that plants help animals? How do plants help you? You can put on a play to show the ways.

You will need:  construction paper yarn crayons tape scissors

Put on a play.

1. Make up a play to show how animals use plants. Show how you use plants too.
2. Make a sign to show what each person in the play is.
3. Put on your play.

Share what you learned.

1. What was fun about your play?
2. Which plant is most important to you? Tell the class why this plant is important to you.

A visit to a greenhouse

As you enter the greenhouse, you feel the warm, moist air. You can smell the soil and flowers. Everywhere you look there are plants. Some plants are just beginning to grow. Other plants are full of bright flowers.

Greenhouse workers must know many things about plants. They have to know which soil is best for plants. They must know how much water plants need. They also have to know how warm to keep plants.

How does a greenhouse work?

1 The roof lets sunlight pass into the greenhouse easily.

4 Some of the heat passes out of the greenhouse.

2 Plants, soil, and other objects inside the greenhouse take in sunlight. As sunlight is taken in, it is changed to heat.

3 The warm objects give off heat that warms the air in the greenhouse. The warm air helps plants grow.

Checkpoint

Greenhouses help people grow flowers and vegetables all year long.

How do greenhouses help you?

Show what you know.

You know a lot about plants and how plants are used. Now you can have a fair to tell other people about plants. What would you show at your plant fair?

Plan your plant fair.

1. Pick a project you will do for the fair.
2. Get what you need for your project.
3. What will you do first?
4. Think about how you will share your project.

Build a model.

Make a model of a plant. Show all the plant parts you learned about. Tell what the plant needs to grow.

Write a song or a poem.

Greet your plant fair visitors with a song or a poem about trees. Your song or poem might tell how trees are used.

Put on a play.

Act out what happens as a plant grows from a seed. Show how the plant can be used.

Share what you know.

1. Share your project.
2. What was the hardest part of your project?
3 What part was the most fun?

Growing and Changing

Growing and Changing

Changes are going on all around you. Everything changes! Living things change as they grow. Even the land and water change.

Growing Up

Growing is changing. How do you think you will look when you grow up? Page **B 4**

Chapter 2
How Animals Grow

Where did that caterpillar go? Some animals go through many changes as they grow.
Page **B 24**

Chapter 3
Changing Things

Don't throw that away!
Recycle it! Page **B 42**

Chapter 1
Growing Up

Do you like to look at your baby pictures? Think of how small you were! Why are baby pictures fun to look at?

You know that you do not look like a baby anymore. You have changed. You have more teeth. You have grown. How else have you changed?

What changes do you see?

1 Bring your baby picture and a newer picture to school.

2 Fold a piece of paper in half. Tape one picture on each side.

3 Write about yourself as a baby.

4 Write about yourself now.

5 **Tell about it.** Tell ways you are the same and ways you have changed.

Ask me what else I want to find out about growing and changing.

How did you change in one year?

Think about how glad you are to be in first grade. Why are you so happy?

You can do many things now that you could not do last year. Maybe you take a bus to school this year. What other changes have happened to you since kindergarten? How have the children in the pictures changed since last year?

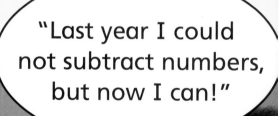

Checkpoint

Write a story. Tell what you do now that you could not do in kindergarten.

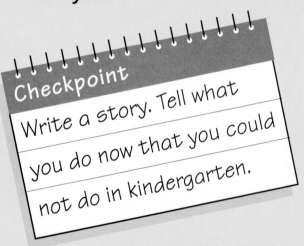

Which teeth have you lost?

Smile! It is school picture day. This picture will look different from your picture taken last year. Your first teeth may be coming out. Larger permanent teeth will take their place.

You will need:

crayons

paper

mirror

Find out about it.

1 Look at your teeth in the mirror.

2 Find the places where teeth are missing. Point to those teeth on the chart.

3 Find any loose teeth. Point to those teeth on the chart.

Write about it.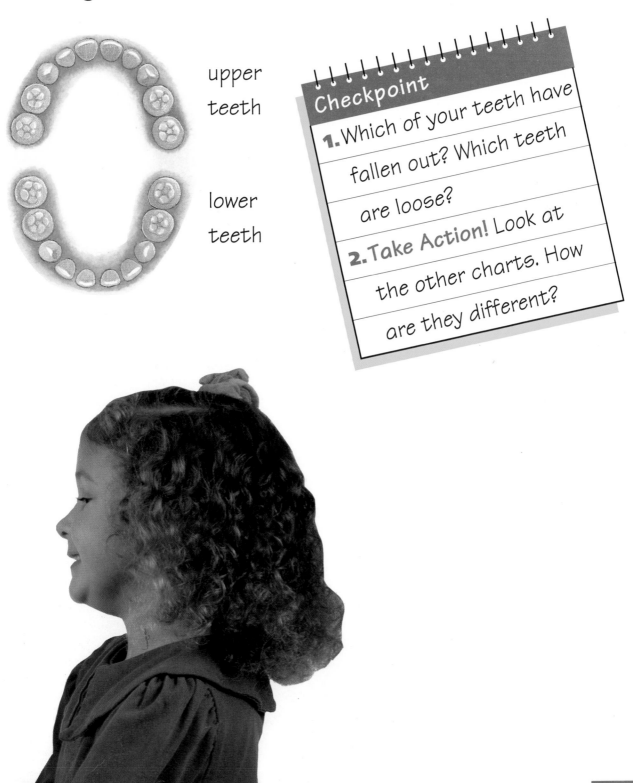

Make a chart like this one. Color the
missing teeth blue. Color the loose teeth red.

upper
teeth

lower
teeth

Checkpoint

1. Which of your teeth have
fallen out? Which teeth
are loose?

2. Take Action! Look at
the other charts. How
are they different?

How do people grow and change?

How will you change as you grow older? As you grow, your size and shape change. You will be able to do new things. You will learn more about getting along with people.

When you are grown up, you will be an adult. How do you think you will look and act as an adult?

Tell about growing up.

You will need: 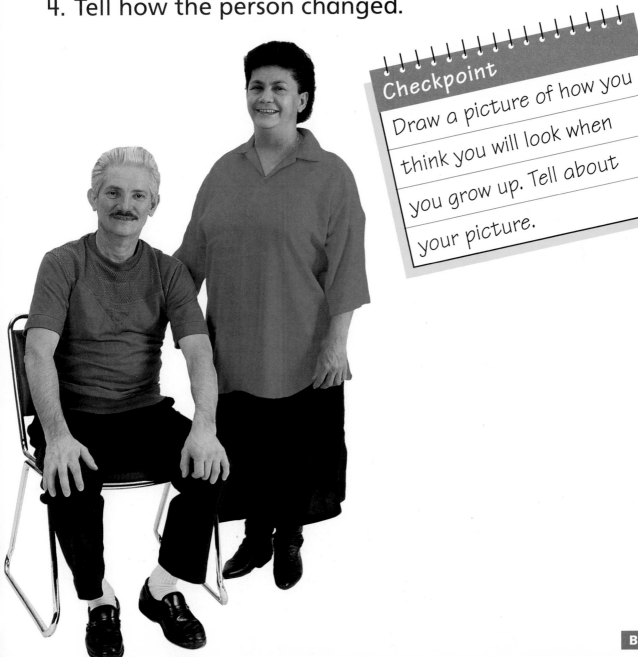 pictures

1. Ask an adult for pictures of herself or himself. The pictures should show the person as a baby, a child, and an adult.
2. Bring the pictures to class.
3. Put the pictures in order. Start with the baby picture.
4. Tell how the person changed.

Checkpoint

Draw a picture of how you think you will look when you grow up. Tell about your picture.

What can help you grow?

As you grow, your body needs certain things. These things keep you healthy. Look at the pictures. Now read about four things that help you grow and be healthy.

Exercise helps you. When you play hard, you get exercise. What games do you play that are good exercise?

Rest helps you. When you sit or sleep you get rest. How do you feel when you do not get enough rest?

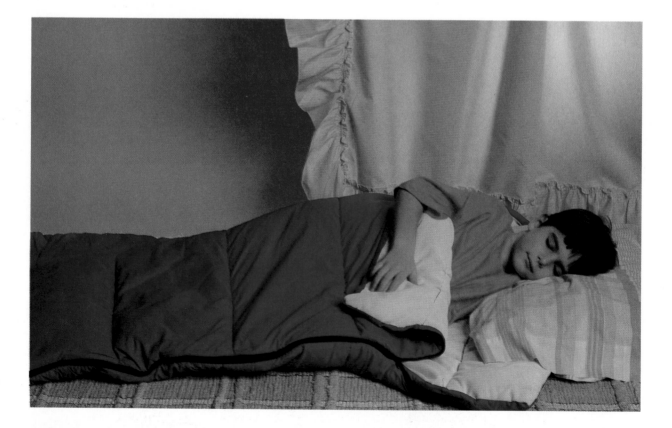

Keeping clean helps you. When you wash you get rid of germs that can make you sick. How do you keep clean?

Food helps you. Some foods are better for you than other foods. What are some foods that help you grow and be healthy?

Checkpoint

Make a poster. Show yourself doing the four things that help you grow and be healthy.

What kinds of foods help you grow?

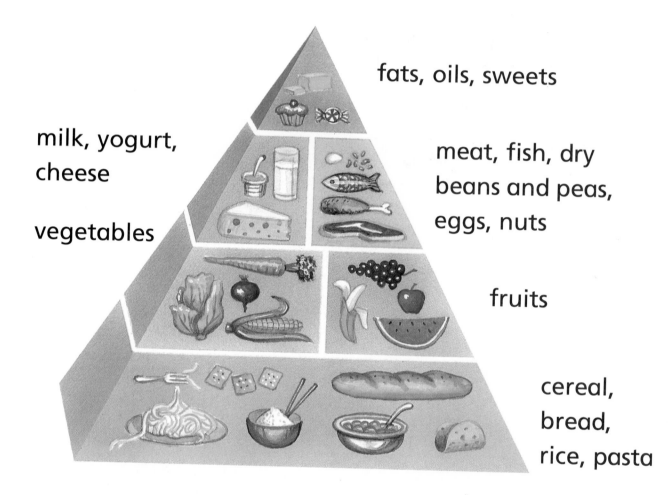

fats, oils, sweets

milk, yogurt, cheese

meat, fish, dry beans and peas, eggs, nuts

vegetables

fruits

cereal, bread, rice, pasta

Do you think your favorite foods help you grow? Different kinds of food help you grow and be healthy. The chart above can help you decide which foods are better for you. You need more of the foods at the bottom of the chart. You need less of the foods near the top.

Make a food chart.

You will need: glue paper ✂ scissors

📖 magazines

1. Look through the magazines.
2. Cut out pictures of different kinds of food.
3. Copy the chart.
4. Glue your pictures in the correct place on the chart.

Checkpoint

Tell why you put the pictures where you did.

What happens to the food you eat?

It's time for lunch! You are very hungry. But what happens to the food you eat? Your body breaks down food and changes it. Then the food can be used by your body.

The way your body changes food is called **digestion.** Digestion starts in your mouth. Teeth break food into small pieces. As you chew, a liquid called **saliva** mixes with food.

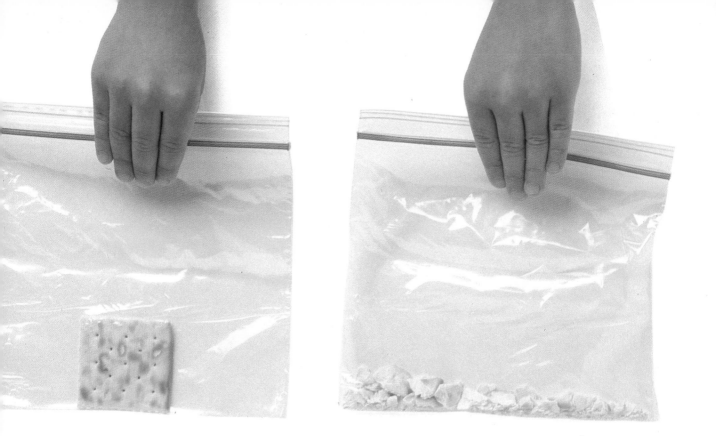

Observe what happens when food is chewed.

You will need: 2 crackers water

2 plastic bags

1. Put 1 cracker into a bag.
2. Put the second cracker into the other bag. Break the cracker into small pieces.
3. Add water to both bags. Seal the bags.
4. Shake each bag 10 times.
5. Look at the 2 crackers. How are they different?

Checkpoint

Tell which bag shows what happens to food in your mouth. Why do you think so?

What happens after you swallow?

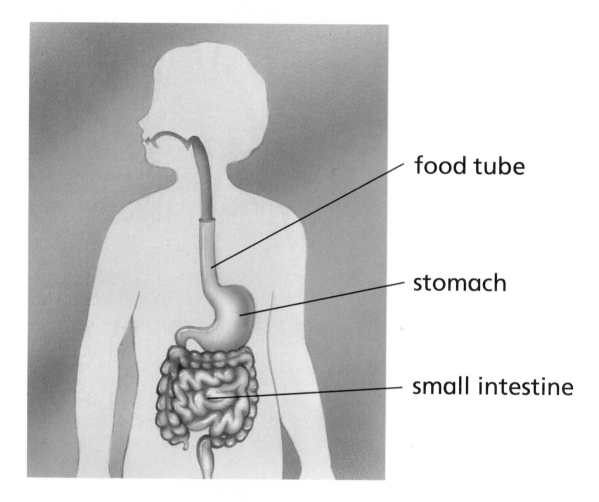

food tube

stomach

small intestine

After you swallow, food is changed more and more. First, it goes down your **food tube** into your stomach. Your **stomach** squeezes food and changes it into a soupy liquid. Then the liquid food moves into the small intestine. Your **small intestine** breaks down the liquid food more. Now the food can be used by your body.

Show the body parts that digest food.

You will need: mural paper paper towel tube balloon string glue crayon

1. Have a classmate trace your outline on the paper.
2. Make a model of the body parts that digest food. Glue the tube, balloon, and string on your outline.
3. Tell which body part looks like a tube. Tell which body part looks like a balloon. Which body part looks like string?

Checkpoint

Use your model to show how food moves through the body. Tell how food changes.

How long does it take to digest food?

Digestion can take a long time. The drawing shows about how long food stays in each part of the body.

1. Look at the drawing. Food takes about 8 seconds to go down the food tube. How long does food stay in the stomach? How long does it stay in the small intestine?

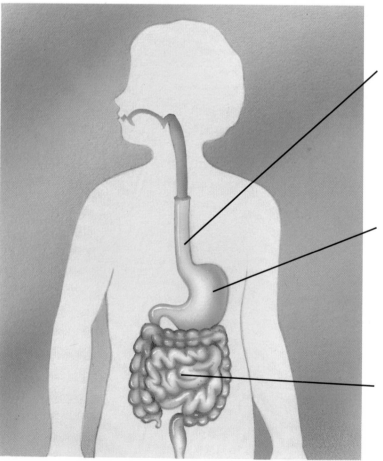

Food is in the food tube about 8 seconds.

Food is in the stomach about 1 to 4 hours.

Food is in the small intestine about 4 hours.

2. Draw a chart like this one.

part of the body	time
food tube	about 8 seconds
stomach	
small intestine	

3. The chart shows about how long food stays in the food tube. On your chart write how long food stays in the stomach. Write how long food stays in the small intestine.

Checkpoint

1. Which part of the body does food go through most quickly?

2. In which parts of the body does food stay about 4 hours?

What did you learn?

My, have you grown! Think of how you have changed. What things help you grow and change? Share what you know by making a book about growing up.

You will need: paper   crayons   pencil

Make a book.

1. Draw a picture of some things you did when you were little.
2. Make a picture of something you will do this year.
3. Draw pictures of you doing the four things that help you grow and be healthy.
4. Draw the parts of the body that help digest your food.
5. Write about your pictures.
6. Make a front and back cover for your book.
7. Put all of your pages together.

HereIAM

Share what you learned.

1. What changes do your pictures show?
2. How do you think you will look when you are in second grade?

B 23

Chapter 2
How Animals Grow

You know that you are growing and changing in many ways. What other things grow and change?

Think about the animals where you live. Maybe you see birds and spiders. Maybe your neighbor has a dog or a cat. All of these animals grow and change. Do animals grow and change in the same ways? Let's find out.

Does a mealworm grow?

1. Place a mealworm on a paper.
2. Mark the beginning and the end of the mealworm. Write day 1 next to it.
3. Do this every 2 days.
4. **Tell about it.** Tell if a mealworm grows. How do you know?

Ask me what else I want to find out about how animals grow and change.

What do animals need to grow?

Animals need four things to live and to grow. One thing animals need is food. Where do you think animals get their food?

Another thing animals need is water. Where might animals find water? Animals also need air and a place to live. You can make a home for mealworms.

Make a home for mealworms.

You will need: apple slice oatmeal

mealworms plastic container with lid

1. Put some oatmeal in the container.
2. Place an apple slice inside the container.
3. Put mealworms into the container and close the lid.
4. Put the home in a warm place away from sunlight.

Checkpoint

Tell how the home has the four things the mealworm needs to live.

How do insects change?

Animals called insects hatch from eggs. Some baby insects look much like the adult insect. One of these insects is the grasshopper.

Some insects change shape as they grow. A mealworm is a **larva**. It will change into a beetle. What shape is the larva? How is the pupa different from the larva? What does the adult look like?

Checkpoint

Tell how a grasshopper changes as it grows. Draw pictures to show how a mealworm changes.

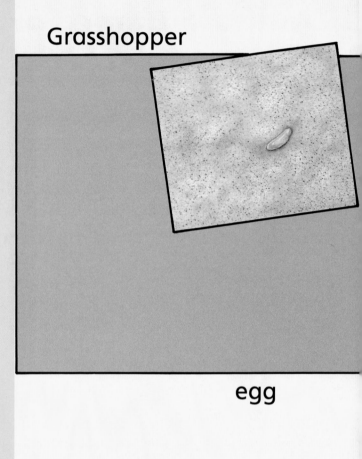

Grasshopper

egg

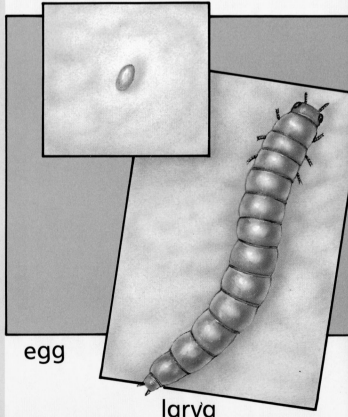

Beetle

egg

larva

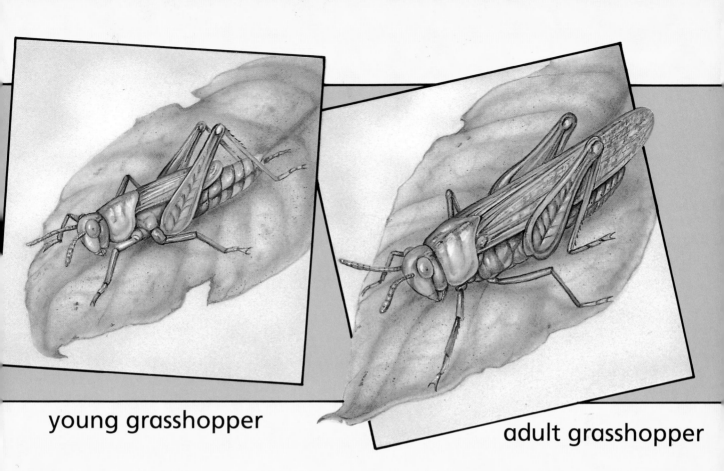

young grasshopper

adult grasshopper

pupa

adult beetle

How do mealworms change?

You found out how mealworms change as they grow. Now let's look at those changes.

You will need:

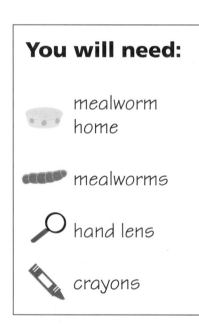

mealworm home

mealworms

hand lens

crayons

Find out about it.

1 Take the lid off the mealworm home.

2 Look at the mealworms with the hand lens.

3 Watch the mealworms for 14 days. Try to find a pupa. Look for adult beetles. Look at the color, size, and shape of each.

Write about it.

Make a chart like this one. Write down or draw the changes in the mealworms.

day	how mealworms look
1	
2	

Checkpoint

1. How did the mealworms change?

2. What change is the most surprising?

3. Take Action! Make a model of a mealworm.

How does a butterfly change?

A butterfly is another insect that changes as it grows. A butterfly hatches from an egg. The larva of a butterfly is called a caterpillar. A caterpillar eats and grows. It changes into a **pupa**. A covering forms around the pupa. Inside the covering, the pupa changes into a butterfly. The butterfly breaks open the covering and crawls out. The butterfly is the adult insect.

caterpillar

pupa

Show how a caterpillar changes into a butterfly.

You will need: cover goggles construction paper

modeling clay ✂ scissors pipe cleaners

1. Shape the clay into a caterpillar.
2. Shape your caterpillar to show how it changes into a pupa.
3. Show how the pupa changes into a butterfly. Put paper wings on the butterfly.
4. Use pipe cleaners for the antennas and legs.

butterfly

Checkpoint

Tell how the changes of a caterpillar and a mealworm are the same. Tell how they are different.

What other animals hatch from eggs?

You learned that insects hatch from eggs. Many other animals also hatch from eggs.

These robins, like other birds, hatch from eggs. A baby bird does not change much as it grows. It looks a lot like its parents. But a baby bird cannot fly. As the bird grows, its feathers change. Most adult birds can fly.

A frog is another animal that hatches from an egg. A baby frog is called a tadpole. Tadpoles change as they grow. Look at the picture. How does the tadpole change?

Checkpoint

Draw two animals that hatch from eggs.

eggs

adult frog

tadpoles

How do some animals grow and change?

Some animals do not hatch from eggs. Some animals grow inside their mother until they are born. Cats and dogs are animals that are born.

The pictures show how rabbits grow and change after they are born. How do the baby rabbits look like their mother? How are they different?

The baby rabbits have just been born.

The rabbits are about a week old.

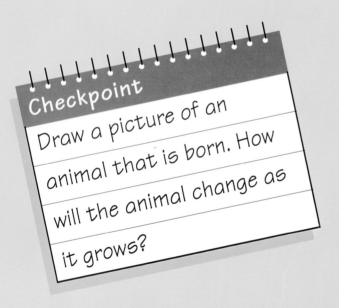

Checkpoint

Draw a picture of an animal that is born. How will the animal change as it grows?

The rabbits are growing and changing.

The rabbit is beginning to look more like the adult.

How does a chicken hatch?

Think about how a caterpillar changes into a butterfly. These changes happen in an order.

The pictures show what happens when a chicken hatches. These things also happen in order.

1. Look at the pictures. In the first picture a chicken is growing inside an egg. What is happening in the second picture?

2. Make a chart like this one.

How does a chicken hatch?	
picture	What is happening?
1	The chicken grows inside the egg.
2	The chicken breaks the shell.
3	
4	

3. The chart shows the first two things that happen when a chicken hatches. Write what is happening in the other pictures.

Checkpoint

1. What happens to the chicken inside the egg?

2. How does the chicken look different in pictures 3 and 4?

What did you learn?

Now you know how some animals grow and change. Make a mobile to show what you learned.

You will need:  paper plates ✏ crayons

 yarn ⟋ hanger

Make a mobile.

1. Draw pictures on a paper plate. Show how a mealworm grows and changes.
2. Tie one end of the string around the hanger. Tie the other end to the plate.
3. Do the same thing for a butterfly, a rabbit, and a frog.

1. How are the changes for the rabbit and the butterfly different?
2. How are the changes for a frog and a person different?

Chapter 3
Changing Things

You know a lot about how living things change. But many other things around you also change. Many things change when you use them. Look at these pictures. Can you find some things that changed?

What things change?

1. Look around your classroom.
2. Find things that change.
3. Make a list of the things you find.
4. Tell how the things change.
5. **Tell about it.** Tell what made the things in your list change.

Ask me what else I want to find out about how things change.

How do you change water?

You know that you can change a lot of things. You even change the water that comes out of your faucet. Look at the pictures to find out how.

What happens to the water after you use it? Water goes through pipes to a place where it is cleaned.

Checkpoint

List ways you use water at home. Tell how you change the water.

Soap suds and bits of food go down the drain.

Water-color paint goes down the drain.

Toothpaste goes down
the drain.

Soap suds and dirt go down
the drain.

How can you clean dirty water?

Dirt and other things can be taken out of water by a filter. Find out how a filter cleans water.

You will need:

bottle

screen

cotton balls

charcoal

sand

tiny stones

dirty water

Find out about it.

1 Turn the top of the bottle upside down. Put it in the bottom part.

2 Place a piece of screen over the opening.

3 Put the cotton balls on top of the screen. Add the charcoal.

4 Place the sand on top of the charcoal. Then add the stones.

5 Pour the dirty water through your filter.

Write about it. ✏️

Make a chart like this one. Write down or draw what you found.

time	how filter looks	how water looks
before filtering		
after filtering		

Checkpoint

1. How did the water change? What changed the water?

2. Take Action! Try to find something else that will filter water.

How do you change land?

Think about things your class throws away. When you throw away trash, you change the land. Read on to find out how.

Most trash is taken to a **landfill**. A landfill is a very big place where trash is buried. Landfills take up a lot of space.

Find things in trash.

You will need: newspapers trash

 plastic bags

1. Cover your hands with plastic bags.
2. Cover the floor with newspaper. Empty the trash onto the floor.
3. Look at the different things in the trash. What kinds of things do you find?

Checkpoint

List the things you found in the trash.

How can you use things again?

Think before you throw away that empty box. Is it really trash? Maybe you can reuse it. When you reuse things, less trash goes to landfills.

Reuse means to use something again. Instead of throwing something away, you use it in a different way. The pictures show things that you can reuse. How is each thing being used in a different way?

You can also help reuse things by giving them away. Then someone else can use things you do not use anymore. So think before you throw away a toy. Who else can use it?

Checkpoint

Tell how something you might throw away can be reused.

How else can you reuse things?

Another way to use things again is to **recycle.** When things are recycled, they are changed. When they are changed, they can be used again.

Metal cans are recycled. The cans are crushed and melted. The recycled metal is used to make new metal things. Maybe you have a toy made of recycled metal.

Sort things to recycle.

You will need: 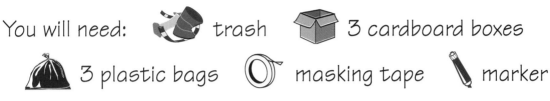 trash   3 cardboard boxes   3 plastic bags   masking tape   marker

1. Put a plastic bag inside each cardboard box. Fold the top of the bag over the edges of the box. Tape the bag in place.

2. Write *paper* on one box. Write *plastic* on the second box. Write *metal* on the third box.

3. Put each kind of trash into its box.

Checkpoint

Tell what things you sorted for recycling.

What else can you recycle?

Think about an apple core or a banana peel from your lunch. Food wastes like these can be recycled to make **compost.**

Compost is made mostly from plant wastes. Leaves, grass, and food scraps make good compost. When these things rot, compost forms. Compost can be added to soil to help plants grow.

Make compost.

You will need: 🫙 plastic jar with cover 🌑 soil
🍈 food scraps 🍃 leaves 🌾 grass
🫙 water 🥢 craft stick

1. Put soil, food scraps, leaves, and grass in the jar.
2. Add a little water. Stir with the craft stick.
3. Cover the jar.
4. Observe the jar every day. How can you tell that the plant wastes are rotting?

Checkpoint

Tell what happens to the plant wastes. How is making compost a way to recycle?

How long does trash stay in a landfill?

You know that most trash is dumped into landfills. But you may not know how long the trash stays there.

Some scientists study trash to find out how old it is. The pictures show four pieces of food found in a landfill.

1. Look at the pictures. The orange peel was about 4 years old when it was found. About how old were the other pieces when they were found?

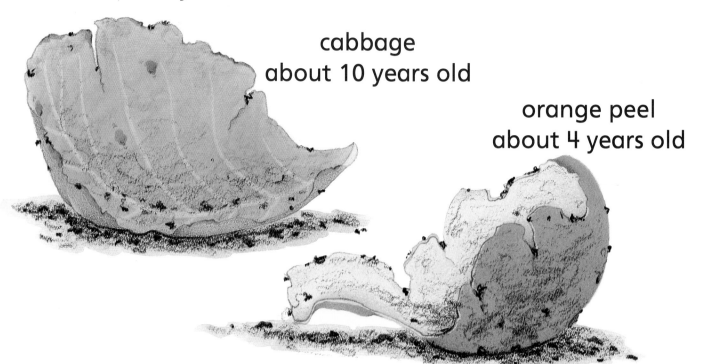

cabbage
about 10 years old

orange peel
about 4 years old

2. Draw a chart like this one.

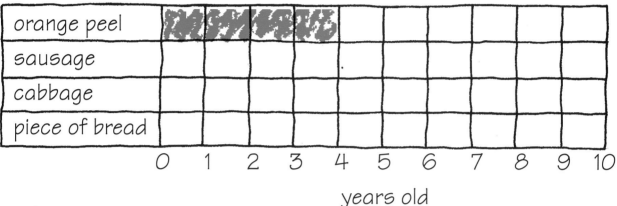

orange peel											
sausage											
cabbage											
piece of bread											

0 1 2 3 4 5 6 7 8 9 10

years old

3. The chart shows about how old the orange peel was. Color your chart to show about how old each of the other foods were.

bread
about 7 years old

sausage
about 4 years old

Checkpoint

1. Which two foods were about the same age when found?

2. Which piece of food was the oldest?

What did you learn?

You found out how you change things. You learned how to reuse and recycle things. You also learned how to make compost. Now make a mural to show what you learned.

You will need:  paper   crayons

Make a mural.

1. Work with a team to plan your mural.
2. Draw things you do that change water.
3. Draw things you do that change land.
4. Draw how you reuse and recycle things.

Share what you learned.

1. What did your mural show about recycling?
2. What can you do so that you make less trash?

A visit to a doctor's office

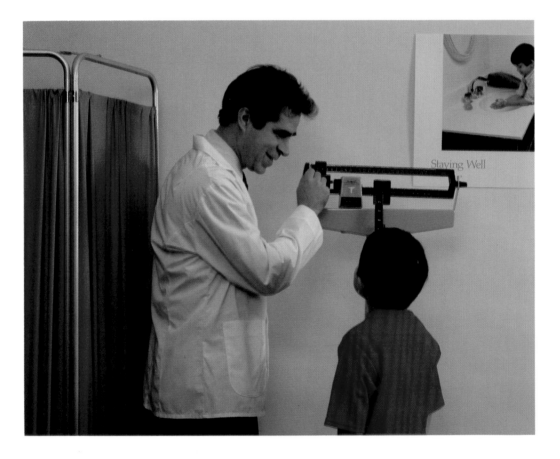

You have probably visited a doctor many times. But today is different. You are here to find out what **nurses** do.

Nurses do things to make sure you are growing. They use a scale to find out what you weigh. Nurses check your heart to see how well it is working. They also give you shots to keep you healthy.

How does a scale work?

3 You use your finger to slide metal weights along the beam.

4 The metal weights balance your weight. The pointer moves to the middle.

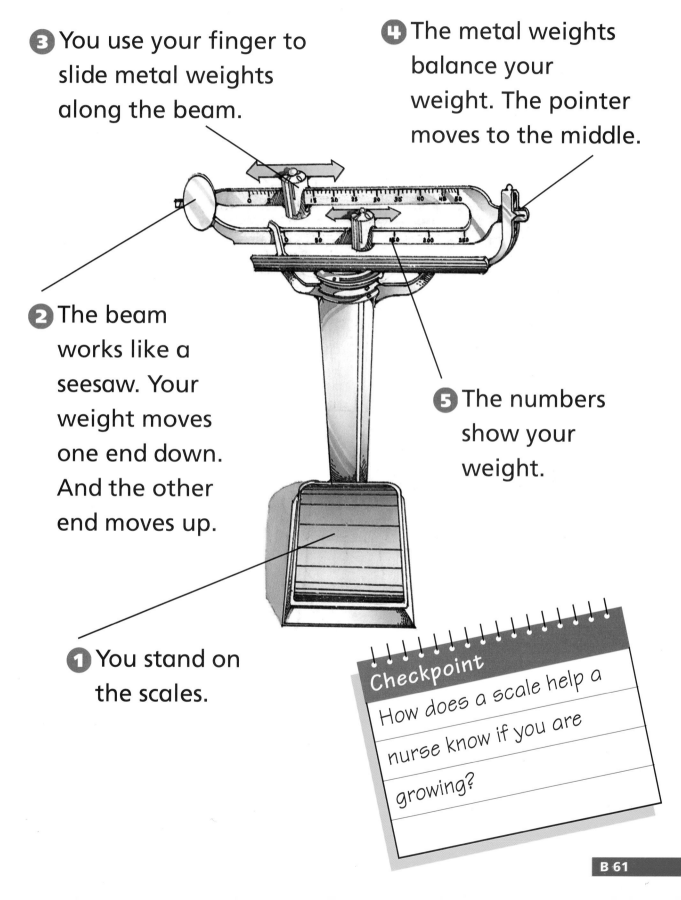

2 The beam works like a seesaw. Your weight moves one end down. And the other end moves up.

5 The numbers show your weight.

1 You stand on the scales.

Checkpoint

How does a scale help a nurse know if you are growing?

Show what you know.

You know a lot about how things change. Now you can show what you know. You can make games about things that change. Then you can play your games.

Plan your game.

1. Pick a game to make.
2. What do you need to make your game?
3. How will you play your game?

Play charades.

Make a list of words you learned. Write each word on a note card. Put the cards into a paper bag. Pick a card from the bag. Act out the word. See if your classmates can guess the word. Take turns.

Play a match game.

Draw yourself as a baby on a note card. Draw yourself as an adult on another card. Do the same thing for five different animals. Place all the cards face-down. Play a match game with a partner.

Play a clue game.

Write five sentences that tell how something changes. The sentences will be clues for a partner. Read one clue at a time. Read clues until your partner guesses the thing that changes.

Share what you know.

1. Share your game.
2. Which games did you like playing?
3. What could you add to your game?

Sound and Light

Sound and Light

Can you imagine being in a world without sound and light? Almost everything around you makes some sound. You need light to see things in the world.

Chapter 1

Hearing and Seeing

Take a listening walk! How can you describe the sounds you hear?
Page C 4

Chapter 2
Making Sounds

Think about your favorite music! How do musical instruments make sound? Page **C 26**

Chapter 3
Light

Turn on the light! Where will the light travel? Page **C 44**

Chapter 1

Hearing and Seeing

Shhh! Do not make a sound. Now listen for sounds around you. What kinds of sounds do you hear? How are the sounds alike? How are the sounds different? Let's find out more about different sounds.

Discover Activity

What sounds do you hear?

1 Get an object you can use to make a sound.

2 Look at the objects your classmates picked. What kind of sound do you think each object will make?

3 Make your sound. Tell how your sound is like another sound.

4 **Tell about it.** Tell which sounds are alike. Tell which sounds are different.

Ask me what else I want to find out about sounds.

What kinds of sounds are there?

Think of a fire drill at school. What kind of sound does the alarm make? Maybe you are surprised by its loud sound. The alarm is loud to warn you. What other loud sounds do you hear at school?

Not all sounds are loud. Some sounds are soft. Whispering is a soft sound. A purring cat makes a soft sound. The words *loud* and *soft* can tell about sounds. What other things make loud and soft sounds?

high sound

low sound

The words *high* and *low* can also tell about sounds. Try whistling. Whistling is a high sound. Now cough. A cough is a low sound. Find the picture of the thing that makes a high sound. What makes a low sound?

Checkpoint

Find something you can use to make a sound. Make the sound. Tell if the sound is loud or soft.

How can you change sounds?

You know sounds can be loud, soft, high, or low. Sounds can change. They can get louder or softer. Sounds can get higher or lower. What makes sounds change?

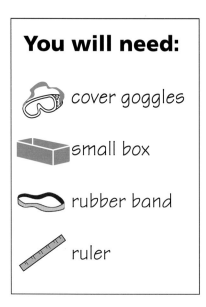

You will need:

cover goggles

small box

rubber band

ruler

Find out about it.

1. Put a rubber band around the box.

2. Pluck the rubber band hard. Is the sound loud or soft?

3. Pluck the rubber band gently. How does the sound change?

4. Put the ruler under the rubber band. Pluck the rubber band.

5. Move the ruler to different places under the rubber band. Pluck the rubber band. What happens?

Write about it. ✏️

Make a chart like this one. Write or draw what you did to make the sound change.

sounds made	what I did
loud	
soft	
high	
low	

Checkpoint

1. How did you make loud sounds? How did you make soft sounds?

2. Take Action! Show how to make high sounds and low sounds.

How can you make sounds softer?

Think of sounds you hear. You may like some sounds. Other sounds are noisy. What makes a sound noisy? Noisy sounds are often loud. They may last a long time.

Loud, noisy sounds can hurt your ears. Think of a time when a loud noise hurt your ears. You might cover your ears when you are around loud sounds. Let's find out why.

Make a sound softer.

You will need: box with lid ticking clock

piece of cloth

1. Put the clock into the box. Close the lid.
2. Listen to the ticking. How loud is it?
3. Open the box. Wrap the cloth around the clock. What do you think will happen to the ticking sound?
4. Close the box and listen.

Checkpoint

Tell how the cloth changed the ticking sound. How might you keep loud sounds from hurting your ears?

How do you hear sound?

You hear sound because sound travels through your ears. Use your finger to follow the sound to the **eardrum** in the picture.

Sound hits the eardrum and makes it move. The moving eardrum makes the inner ear parts move. These moving ear parts send out sound messages. The sound messages follow a path to the brain. Then you hear the sound.

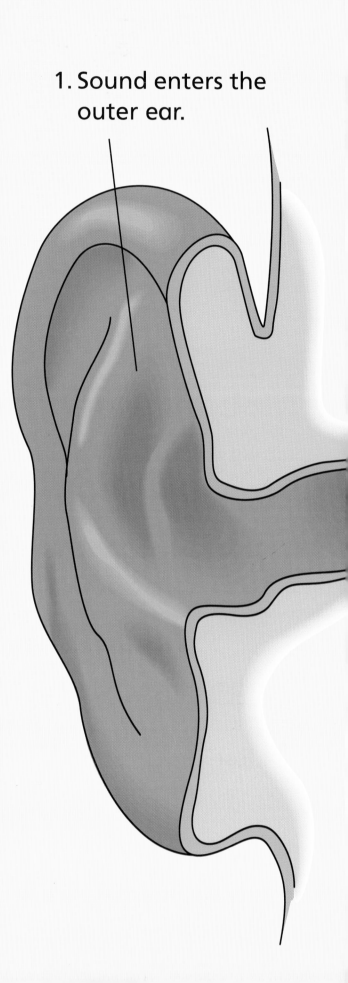

1. Sound enters the outer ear.

Checkpoint

Tell how you hear a sound.

Use your finger to trace the path sound takes in the picture.

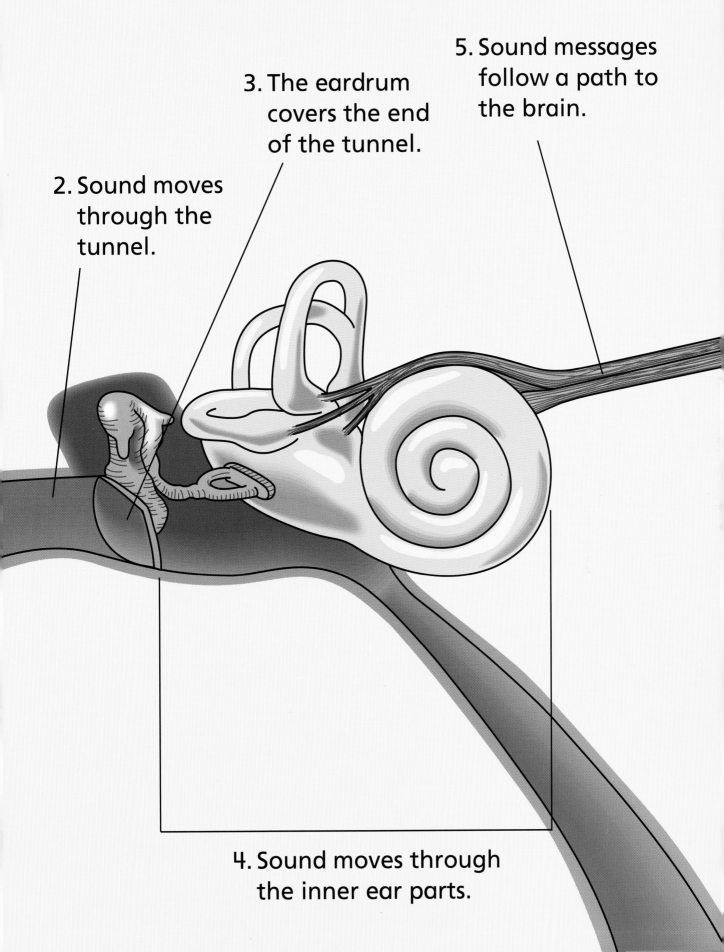

2. Sound moves through the tunnel.

3. The eardrum covers the end of the tunnel.

5. Sound messages follow a path to the brain.

4. Sound moves through the inner ear parts.

Do you hear better with two ears?

Think about what happens when you hear a cricket chirping. You can not see it. But you can hear it. How do you use your ears to find the cricket?

You will need:

paper cup

cotton

ticking clock

Find out about it.

1 Stand in the middle of the room. Close your eyes. Have a classmate hide the clock.

2 Listen for the ticking sound. Point to where the clock is hidden. How close was your guess?

3 Fill the paper cup with cotton. Put the cup over one ear.

4 Do numbers 1 and 2 again. How close was your guess this time?

Write about it.

Make a chart like this one. Write down what you found out.

number of ears used	How easy was the clock to find?
2 ears	
1 ear	

Checkpoint

1. Was it easier to find the clock with one ear or two ears? Why?

2. Take Action! Find out if two ears help you hear sounds farther away.

What can you see without light?

Pretend you are walking into a dark room. How well can you see? Suddenly the lights are turned on. How does light change what you see?

Look at things in the dark.

You will need:  shoe box with lid

small toy book

1. Put the toy in the box. Put the lid on.
2. Look through the small hole in the end of the box. What do you see?
3. Use the book to cover the hole in the lid. What do you think you will be able to see in the box?
4. Look through the small hole in the end of the box again. What do you see?

Checkpoint

Draw a picture. Show what you saw each time you looked into the box. Tell how light changes what you see.

How do you see things?

You see things because light travels through your eyes. Use your finger to follow the light to the back of the eye in the picture.

Light hits the back of the eye. Messages are sent out from the eye. The messages follow a path to the brain. When the messages get to the brain, you see.

3. Light hits the back of the eye.

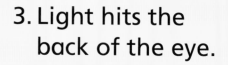

4. Messages from the back of the eye follow a path to the brain.

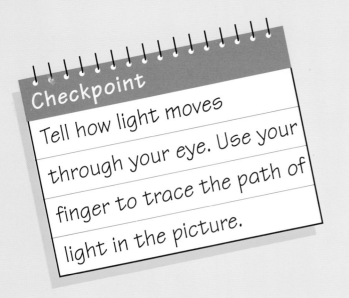

Checkpoint

Tell how light moves through your eye. Use your finger to trace the path of light in the picture.

2. Light moves through the **lens.**

1. Light enters the eye through a small opening called the **pupil.**

Do you see better with two eyes?

You may have seen a picture of a pirate. Was the pirate wearing a patch over one eye? Suppose you needed an eye patch. What would happen if you used just one eye to see?

You will need:

cover goggles

ball

paper

tape

Find out about it.

1. Stand facing a partner. Each of you take 3 giant steps backward.

2. Have your partner toss you a ball 10 times. Count how many times you catch it.

3. Tape paper to the outside of one side of the cover goggles.

4. Put on the goggles. Have your partner toss you the ball 10 times. Count the times you catch the ball.

Write about it.

Make a chart like this one. Write how many times you catch the ball.

number of eyes used	number of times ball was caught
2 eyes	
1 eye	

Checkpoint

1. In which try did you catch more balls? Why?

2. Take Action! Try to do other things while one eye is covered. Tell what happens.

How can light change your pupils?

Remember when you traced the path of light through the eye? Light gets into the eye through the pupil. Did you know that your pupils can change size? They get larger or smaller when light hits them.

1. Look at the eyes of a person in a room with little light. The pupils are large.
2. Look at the eyes of a person in a room with bright light. The pupils are small.

little light

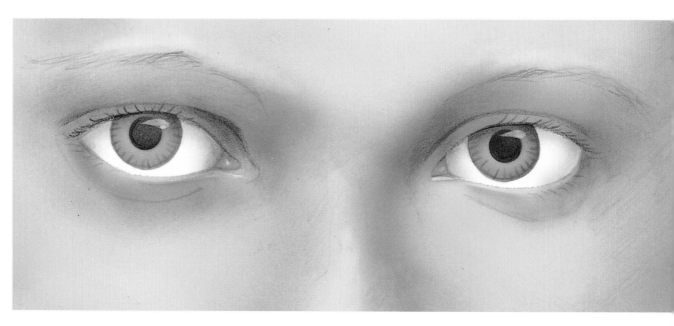

3. Draw a chart like this one.

place	how much light	how pupil looks
outside on a sunny day		
outside at night		

4. Write how much light each place has.
5. Draw a different eye for each row. Show how your pupil will look in the different lights.

Checkpoint
1. Tell where your pupils will be large.
2. When might your pupils get smaller?

bright light

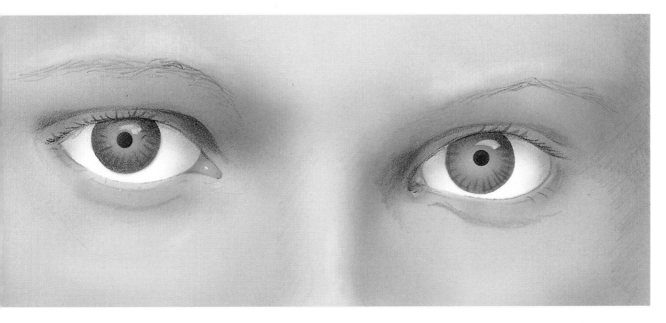

What did you learn?

Now you know about different kinds of sounds. You know how you hear. You also know how you see. You can make a book to show what you have learned.

You will need: 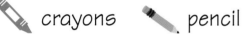 construction paper ☐ paper

🖍 crayons ✏ pencil

Make a book.

1. Draw pictures to show four things you learned.
2. Write about your pictures.
3. Put your pictures together to make a book.
4. Use construction paper. Make a cover for your book.
5. Share your book with a classmate.

eye

Share what you learned.

1. Why did you choose the four things you did?

2. What is your favorite picture in your book? Tell why.

Chapter 2
Making Sounds

Ding-ding. Clickety-clack. Chug-chug-chug. Whrrr. Screeech! Yikes! Welcome to the carnival! You hear many sounds. Children laugh and shout. Game bells ring. Music plays. The rides rumble, squeak, and clatter. How are all of these sounds made? Let's find out.

How can you make sounds?

1 Stretch a rubber band around your fingers.

2 Pluck or strum the rubber band. What did you see happen to the rubber band?

3 **Tell about it.** Tell how you think the sound is made.

Ask me what else I want to find out about how sounds are made.

What makes sounds?

When an object moves back and forth quickly, it **vibrates.** As the object vibrates, it makes **sound.** You heard the sounds made by the rubber band. You also saw the rubber band vibrate. Sometimes you can feel when an object vibrates. Find out how.

Find what vibrates.

You will need: cover goggles balloon

1. Blow up the balloon. Hold the balloon closed with your fingers.
2. Place your fingers on both sides of the opening in the balloon. Pull both sides and let some air out. What happens?
3. Make different sounds. What vibrates when the sounds are made?

Checkpoint

Tell how you know what vibrates when you made the sounds. What made the sounds?

Does sound travel through things?

You can hear people talking across a room. How do these sounds travel to your ear? Let's find out what sound travels through.

You will need:

plastic bags

pencil with eraser

water

wood

Find out about it.

1 Get three sealed plastic bags.

2 Put the bag with air on a table. Put one ear on the bag. Then put your hand over your other ear.

3 Have a classmate softly tap the pencil on the table. What do you hear?

4 Do the same thing with the bag with water and the bag with wood. What do you hear?

Write about it.

Make a chart like this one. Write how well you hear the tapping sound.

What is in the bag?	How well do I hear?
air	
water	
wood	

Checkpoint

1. Did you hear the sound best through air, water, or wood?

2. Take Action! Find other objects that sound travels through.

How does sound travel?

You are playing outside. Suddenly, a bird in a tree starts to sing loudly. You hear the singing because sound travels through the air.

The sounds of the bird make the air vibrate. The sounds travel out in all directions from the bird. When the sounds reach your ears, you hear the sounds.

You know you can hear sounds through wood and through water. You hear these sounds because sounds make the wood and the water vibrate.

Checkpoint

Tell a classmate how sound travels through the air.

Will sound travel through a string?

You learned that sound can travel through air, water, and wood. Do you think that sound can travel through a string?

You will need:

 string telephone

Find out about it.

1 Work with a partner. Use the string telephone.

2 Step back from your partner. Let the string hang loosely between you.

3 Hold one cup over your ear. Listen as your partner whispers into the other cup.

4 Step back from your partner until the string is tight.

5 Listen again as your partner whispers into the other cup.

Write about it.

Make a chart like this one. Write yes or no for your answers.

string	Can you hear your partner?
loose string	
stretched string	

Checkpoint

1. Does sound travel through a loose string? How do you know?

2. Take Action! Find out how far sound travels through a string.

How can you hear sound better?

Think about some soft sounds you can hardly hear. What can help you hear the sounds better? Think about your ear. The size and shape of your ear is good for catching sounds.

The ear trumpet in the picture is good for catching sounds too. Find out if an ear trumpet can help you hear better.

Use an ear trumpet.

You will need: masking tape construction paper

 pencil ▮ metal object

1. Roll a piece of paper into a cone.
2. Make the cone so that the small end fits over your ear.
3. Tape the cone together.
4. Have your partner tap a pencil on a metal object.
5. Put the small end of the ear trumpet over your ear. Listen to the sound.
6. Take the ear trumpet away from your ear. Listen to the sound.

Checkpoint

Tell how you know that the ear trumpet helps you hear better. Tell how it helps you hear better.

How can you make music?

You are watching a parade. Many kinds of instruments are being played. You hear loud, high sounds. There are soft, low sounds too. The sounds all come together to make music.

The children are playing instruments they made. You can make your own instrument. Look at what you might use. Make your favorite instrument.

Checkpoint

Show how you play your instrument. Tell what vibrates when you play a note.

shaker

guitar

flute

drum

What sounds do bottle pipes make?

When you blow across a bottle the air inside vibrates. You can make low to high sounds with a bottle pipe. Bottles with a lot of air make low sounds. Bottles with a little air make high sounds.

1. Look at the bottle pipes. Which bottle makes the lowest sound? Which bottle makes the highest sound?

1   2   3   4   5   6

2. Draw a chart like this one.

5	3	5	5	3		
■	■	■	■	■		
Rain,	rain	go	a-	way,		

5	5	3	6	5	5	3
■	■	■	■	■	■	■
Come	a-	gain	a-	noth-	er	day.

4	2	4	4	2		
□	□	□	□	□		
Rain,	rain	go	a-	way,		

5	6	5	4	3	2	1
□	□	□	□	□	□	□
All	the	chil-	dren	want	to	play.

3. The chart shows which bottles to use to play the song. The colors help you match the numbers with the bottles.

4. Color your chart for the last two lines of the song.

Checkpoint

1. What bottles did you use for the first line?

2. What other song would you like to play?

What did you learn?

You now know how sounds are made. You also know how sounds travel through air, water, and different objects. Pretend you work for a person who makes movies. Your job is to help make sounds for the movie.

You will need:  objects that make sound

children's story

Make movie sounds.

1. Listen to a story.
2. List what sounds are in the story.
3. Choose one sound you want to make.
4. Decide how you can make that sound. Use objects from your school or home.
5. Listen to the story again. Make the sound when your part is read.
6. Tape-record the story with the sounds.

Share what you learned.

1. What sound did you make? How did you make the sound?
2. Which movie sound was most like the real sound?

Chapter 3
Light

Do you like to play with a flashlight? Maybe you like to shine the light on different things. It is fun to see what happens.

Think about what happens when you shine the light on a wall. How does light travel from the flashlight to the wall?

How does light travel?

1. Get a flashlight and 2 note cards.
2. Stand the cards in a row. Use clay to hold up the cards. Make sure the holes are lined up.
3. Shine a light through the hole in the first card. What do you see?
4. Move the second card out of line.
5. Shine a light through the hole in the first card again. Now what do you see?
6. **Tell about it.** Tell what happens to the light each time.

Ask me what else I want to find out about light.

What can light move through?

Suppose you put a book over a flashlight. Would the light move through the book? Light can move through some things. Think about your home. Sunlight comes in through the glass windows. Only a little light can move through window shades or curtains. No light can move through the walls. What kinds of things does light move through best?

Observe what light moves through.

You will need:  flashlight · wax paper · clear plastic wrap · cardboard

1. Work with a partner. Turn off the lights.
2. Shine the flashlight on a wall.
3. Put the plastic wrap in front of the flashlight. How well can you see the light on the wall?
4. Put the wax paper in front of the flashlight. How well can you see the light on the wall?
5. Do the same thing with the cardboard.

Checkpoint

Tell how much light moves through each object. Which object stops the most light?

How can you make a shadow?

Because light moves in straight lines, you can make a shadow with your hands. The light hits your hands but cannot go through them. A **shadow** forms behind your hands where the light cannot go.

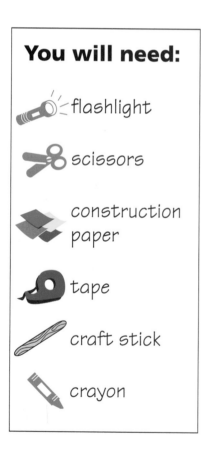

You will need:

flashlight

scissors

construction paper

tape

craft stick

crayon

Find out about it.

1 Draw an animal shape on the paper. Cut out the shape.

2 Tape the shape to a craft stick.

3 Shine the flashlight on a wall.

4 Hold your animal puppet close to the front of the flashlight. Look at the shadow.

5 Move the puppet away from the light. What happens to the shadow?

Write about it.

Make a chart like this one. Write what happens to the shadow.

Where is the puppet?	What happens to the shadow?
close to flashlight	
away from flashlight	

Checkpoint

1. How did you make the shadow big?

2. Take Action! Find out what happens to the shadow if you cut a hole in the puppet.

Can you make light bounce?

When you drop a ball on a sidewalk it bounces back to you. When light hits an object some of the light bounces back. Light bounces best when it hits smooth, shiny objects. A mirror is smooth and shiny.

Make a mirror.

You will need: cardboard square tape

clear plastic square   aluminum foil square

flashlight

1. Put the foil square on top of the cardboard. Make sure the shiny side faces up.
2. Put the clear plastic on top of the foil.
3. Tape the squares together at each side.
4. Shine the flashlight on your mirror.
5. Move the mirror so the light bounces to different parts of the room.

Checkpoint

Tell where the light bounces after it hits your mirror. Why does this happen?

How can objects look different?

Sometimes an object looks different than it really is. The glass lens in the picture makes the stamp look bigger.

Curved mirrors also make you look different. Some make you look taller. Others make you look big and wide.

How does the arm look different in water? How does the penny in the water look different?

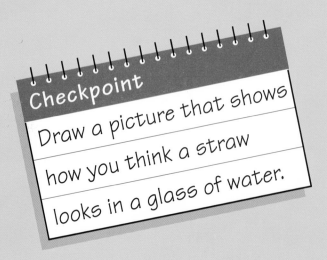

What makes a rainbow?

Do you know that light is really made up of many colors? You can see these colors. Look at the picture of the prism. What happens as the light moves through the prism?

As the light moves through the prism, the colors separate. Then you see the different colors.

The same thing happens when you see a rainbow. Sunlight moves through drops of water in the air. The drops of water act like little prisms. They separate the colors in light. That is why you see the different colors in the rainbow.

Checkpoint

Tell why you see the different colors in a rainbow.

What colors do you see in a rainbow?

Close your eyes. Think of the colors you see in a rainbow. Do you know that the same colors are in all rainbows? The colors are in the same order.

1. Look at the drawing of a rainbow. Start at the top and name the colors.

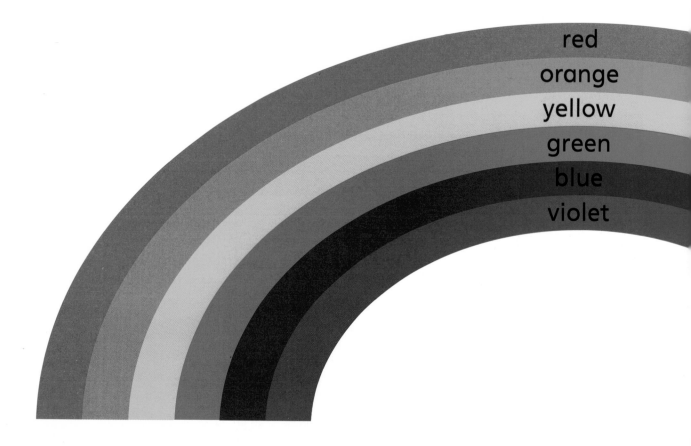

red
orange
yellow
green
blue
violet

2. Draw a chart like this one.

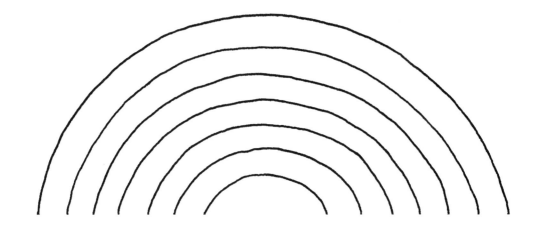

3. Color the chart to look like a rainbow. Put the colors in the right order.

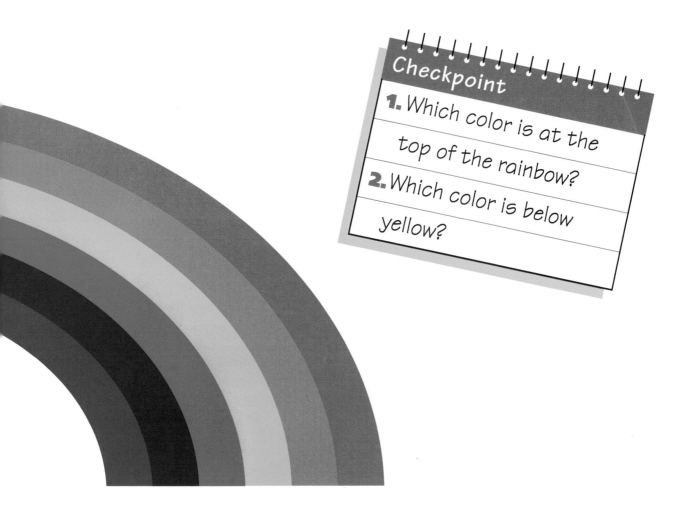

Checkpoint

1. Which color is at the top of the rainbow?
2. Which color is below yellow?

What did you learn?

Now you know a lot about light. You know that light moves in a straight line. Light can bounce. It can go through some things. But it cannot go through everything. Pretend you are putting on a television show about light.

Make a TV show.

You will need:  mirror   hand lens   flashlight   puppets   wax paper   cardboard   plastic wrap   water   clear plastic cup   straw

1. Work as a team. Talk about what you liked learning about light.
2. Plan a 5 minute TV show about what you learned.
3. Plan to do one activity about light as part of the show.
4. Practice your show. Put on your show for your class.

Share what you learned.

1. What activity did you use in your show?
2. What is the most fun thing you learned about light?

A visit to a photo studio

You sit very still and look at the camera. You smile your biggest smile. Where are you? You are at a photo studio. The person who is taking your picture is called a **photographer**.

Photographers need to know how a camera works. They also need to know a lot about light. To take a good picture, photographers need the right amount of light.

How does a camera work?

① The viewfinder shows what will be in the picture.

② The lens allows light to enter the camera.

③ The shutter opens and closes to allow light to hit the film.

Checkpoint

Find some pictures in this book that you think were taken in a photo studio.

Show what you know.

Your world is filled with sound and light. Your ears and eyes help you hear and see the world around you. Let's celebrate sound and light. Use what you know to put on a sound and light show.

Plan a festival.

1. Pick a show you would like to do.
2. What do you need to do your show?
3. What will you do first?
4. Think about how your show will look in the festival.

Make a puppet show.

Make shadow puppets and a stage. Show how your puppets act when they hear loud and soft sounds.

Put on a play.

Put on a play that shows what your eyes and ears do. How can you use light and sound in your play?

Play and sing a song.

Write words for a song about what light does. Make an instrument to play as you sing your song.

Share what you know.

1. Share your project.
2. What do the other shows tell you?
3. What was fun about doing your show?

Weather

Weather

The weather is changing most of the time. The air gets colder or warmer. The sun may be shining one day. Then the next day, there's a snowstorm!

Chapter 1

Describing Weather

Is it cold or warm outside? How can you measure air temperature to find out? Page **D 4**

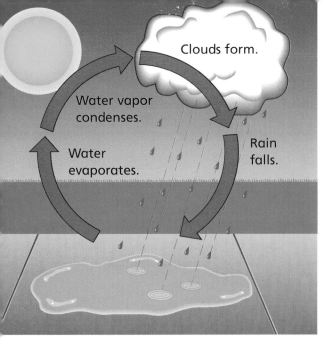

Clouds form.

Water vapor condenses.

Water evaporates.

Rain falls.

Chapter 2

Air, Water, and Weather

Clouds may look like piles of cotton in the sky. But clouds are really tiny drops of water in the air! Page **D 22**

Chapter 3

Weather and You

Rain, rain go away! When was the last time rain made you change your plans? Page **D 46**

Chapter 1
Describing Weather

You wake up. It is Saturday morning! You want to play outside. Quick, run to the window. What kind of weather do you want to see?

Tell what your weather is like today. Use words that tell about the weather. Some words are *cloudy* and *sunny*. What is your favorite weather?

Discover Activity

What words tell about weather?

1. Think of words that tell what the weather is like.
2. Write the words on chart paper.
3. Think of a picture that tells about each word. Draw that picture next to each word.
4. **Tell about it.** Tell what kind of weather each picture shows.

Ask me what else I want to find out about weather.

How can weather change?

What was the weather like when you left for school this morning? The weather may be very different when you go home this afternoon.

Weather can change during the day. Have you seen weather change from cloudy to sunny? What other weather changes have you seen during a day?

Chart your weather for a day.

You will need: paper ✏️ crayons

1. Fold your paper into three parts. Write *morning* at the top of one part. Do the same for *noon* and *afternoon.*

2. Observe the weather in the morning. Under the word *morning,* write words that tell about the weather. Draw a picture to go with each word.

3. Do the same thing for noon and for afternoon.

Checkpoint

Tell how the weather changed during the day.

morning noon afternoon

What helps you tell about weather?

The sun is shining. But is the air warm? Can you go outside without a jacket? You may want to find out what the temperature is. **Temperature** tells how warm the air is.

You can use a **thermometer** to find the temperature. A thermometer has a tube with a liquid in it. As the air gets warmer, the liquid moves up the tube. What happens to the liquid when the air gets cooler?

warm air   cold air

Measure air temperature.

You will need: thermometer

1. Read a thermometer in the classroom.
2. Go outside. Is it colder or warmer?
3. Leave the thermometer outside for 5 minutes. Did the liquid go up or down from the inside temperature?
4. Read the temperature on the thermometer.

Checkpoint

Write about how a thermometer helps you tell about weather.

How can you measure wind?

Hold your hand out in front of you. Wave your hand very fast. What you feel on your hand is moving air. The moving air is called **wind.**

Wind can blow softly. Wind can also blow hard. You can make a tool that shows how hard the wind blows.

Make a tool to measure wind.

You will need:  drinking straw ⦉ tissue paper

✂ scissors 📼 tape

1. Cut out a paper flag. Tape it to the end of a straw.
2. Blow softly on the flag. Draw a picture to show what happens to the flag.
3. Blow hard. Draw a picture to show what happens to the flag.
4. Go outside and measure the wind. Hold up the flag. What happens to it?

Checkpoint

Tell if the wind is blowing hard or soft today.

How hard can wind blow?

You can measure how hard wind blows. You can also tell by looking out a window. Watch how the wind makes things move.

Picture 1 shows no wind. How can you tell? Picture 2 shows wind blowing softly. What is happening in this picture? Look at picture 3 and picture 4. In which picture is the wind blowing harder? How can you tell?

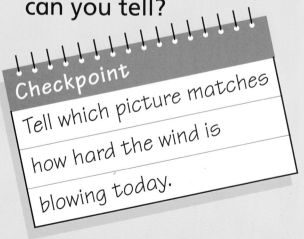

Checkpoint

Tell which picture matches how hard the wind is blowing today.

picture 1

picture 2

picture 3

picture 4

How can you measure rainfall?

Have you ever watched it rain? Sometimes it rains a lot. Other times, it only rains a little. You can measure rainfall with a rain gauge.

You will need:

masking tape

clear jar

crayons

ruler

Find out about it.

1 Make a rain gauge. Cut a strip of tape as long as the jar.

2 Draw lines on the tape 1 centimeter apart.

3 Start with number 1. Number the lines on the tape from bottom to top.

4 Put the tape on the jar.

5 Measure the rain on 5 rainy days.

Write about it.

Make a chart like this one. Write down how much rain falls each day.

day	how much rain
1	cm
2	cm
3	cm
4	cm
5	cm

Checkpoint

1. Which day had the most rain? How can you tell?

2. Take Action! Measure the rainfall for 5 or more days. Make a chart to show the rainfall.

What happens during a storm?

It is a sunny, summer day. Then you see big dark clouds in the sky. After a while, you can't see the sun. What do you think might happen next?

dark clouds

lightning

Lightning flashes in the sky. Loud cracks of thunder soon follow. Then comes hard wind and pouring rain. A thunderstorm is here! The pictures show some things that happen in a thunderstorm. What other things might happen?

wind

Checkpoint

Tell a story about a thunderstorm you remember. What did you see? What did you feel? What did you hear?

rain

How can you show rainfall?

You learned that it rains hard during a thunderstorm. Now find out how to show how much rain falls during a storm. You can make a chart to show this.

1. Look at the rain gauge for thunderstorm A. Two centimeters of rain fell during thunderstorm A.

2. How much rain fell during thunderstorm B?

3. How much rain fell during thunderstorm C?

thunderstorm A

centimeters

10
9
8
7
6
5
4
3
2
1

thunderstorm B

centimeters

10
9
8
7
6
5
4
3
2
1

thunderstorm C

centimeters

10
9
8
7
6
5
4
3
2
1

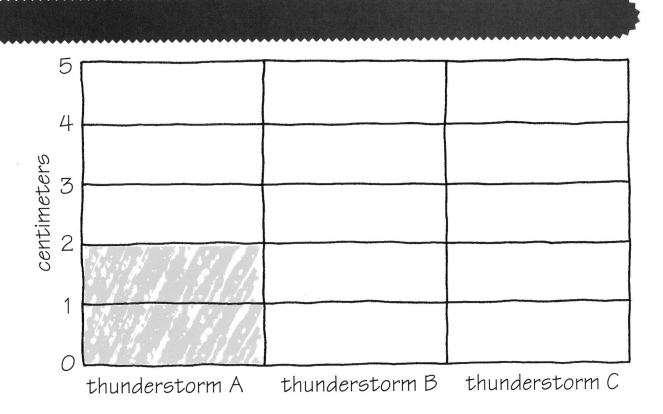

4. Draw a chart like this one. Each part of the chart shows how much rain fell during a storm.

5. Two centimeters of rain are colored in for thunderstorm A.

6. Color in your chart to show how much rain fell in storm B and storm C.

Checkpoint

1. How much rain fell in thunderstorm B?

2. In which storm did the most rain fall?

What did you learn?

You can look at weather and talk about it. You can measure temperature and rainfall. A weather chart will help you see how weather changes each day.

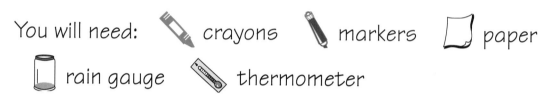

You will need: crayons   markers   paper   rain gauge   thermometer

Make a weather chart.

1. Draw a chart like the one on the next page. Write weather words to tell about each day.
2. Read your thermometer. Write the temperature.
3. Read your rain gauge. Write how much rain fell.
4. Draw a flag that shows how hard the wind is blowing.

Weather Chart

What is the weather like?	day 1	day 2	day 3	day 4	day 5
	sunny				
What is the temperature?					
How much rain fell?					
How hard is the wind blowing?					

Share what you learned.

1. What was the temperature on day 1?
2. How were day 2 and day 5 different?
3. Which days were good days to play outside?

Chapter 2
Air, Water, and Weather

Get ready! Get set! Go! The big, bright balloons lift off the ground. Soon they are higher than the tallest trees and buildings!

Maybe you know that air can lift things like these balloons. What else do you know about air? Do you know that air is an important part of weather? Let's find out how.

Discover Activity

Where is air?

1. Hold a plastic bag open with your hands.
2. Wave the bag back and forth.
3. Seal the bag. Do you see anything inside? Do you feel anything inside?
4. **Tell about it.** Tell what you think is in the bag. Where did it come from?

Ask me what else I want to find out about air and weather.

Is there water in the air?

You learned where air is. Now find out what is in air. Does air have water in it? You cannot see the water. How can you find out if water is there?

You will need:

can

food coloring

plastic wrap

ice

water

masking tape

Find out about it.

1 Fill the can with ice and water.

2 Add 2 or 3 drops of food coloring.

3 Cover the top of the can with plastic wrap. Tape the plastic wrap to the can. Wait 5 minutes.

4 Look at the can. What changes do you see on the outside of the can?

Write about it. ✏️

Make a chart like this one. Draw or write what you see.

time	how can looks
at start	
after 5 minutes	

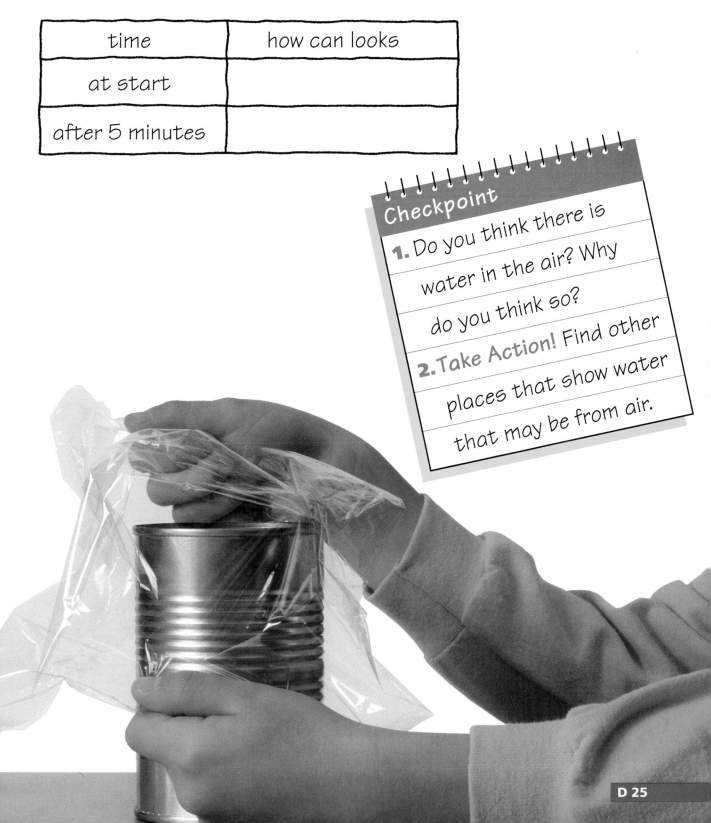

Checkpoint

1. Do you think there is water in the air? Why do you think so?

2. Take Action! Find other places that show water that may be from air.

Where is water in the air?

You can see and feel the water you drink. But you cannot see water in the air. Water in the air is in a form of water called **water vapor.** You cannot see water vapor.

Remember the drops of liquid water on the cold can? They came out of the air. Here is how they formed. The cold can cools the water vapor in the air around the can. When water vapor cools, it **condenses.** It changes from water vapor to liquid water.

Look at the dew drops on the spider web.
The drops form when water vapor in the air
cools. The cool water vapor condenses on
the threads of the web.

Checkpoint

Tell what happens when
water vapor condenses.

How does water get into the air?

You found out that water is in the air. You saw how the water condenses and comes out of the air. But how does water get into the air?

Have you ever seen a puddle dry up in the sun? If so, you have seen water **evaporate.** The liquid water changes to water vapor. Water goes into the air when it evaporates. Do this activity to watch water evaporate.

Watch water evaporate.

You will need:  water   paintbrush

1. Quickly paint a water picture on the chalkboard.
2. Watch what happens to your picture.

Checkpoint

Tell what happens to your picture. Where do you think the water goes?

What makes water go into the air faster?

Sometimes a puddle dries up quickly. Sometimes a puddle dries more slowly. Why does this happen? Let's find out!

You will need:

2 paper towels

water

dropper

cardboard

Find out about it.

1 Put one paper towel at one end of a table. Put another paper towel at the other end of the table.

2 Put a few drops of water on each paper towel.

3 Fan one of the paper towels with the cardboard. Watch what happens to the paper towels. Notice how fast each one dries.

Write about it.

Make a chart like this one. Write *1* next to the paper towel that dries first. Write *2* next to the paper towel that dries last.

paper towels	how fast towels dried
fanned	
not fanned	

Checkpoint

1. Which towel dried first? Why did it dry first?

2. Take Action! Draw a picture of the weather that might help a puddle evaporate fast.

What else makes water evaporate?

You made water on the towel evaporate faster. You used moving air. You know that wind is moving air. Windy weather makes water evaporate faster. What other kind of weather could make water evaporate faster? Sunlight might do it! How could you find out? Try this activity.

Make a towel dry faster.

You will need:  2 paper towels   water

  dropper

1. Put one paper towel in sunlight.
2. Put the other paper towel in shade.
3. Put a few drops of water on each paper towel. Watch what happens to the paper towels.

Checkpoint

Tell which paper towel dried first. Tell what kind of weather you think will make things dry fast.

How can water condense?

You know that water from a puddle evaporates into the air. It becomes water vapor. The water vapor moves into the air. When the water vapor rises high in the sky, it cools. Then the water vapor condenses to form tiny water drops in the sky. You can make water evaporate and condense.

Make water evaporate and condense.

You will need: cup with water   plastic bag

1. Put the cup in a plastic bag. Put the bag on a table.
2. Close the bag part way.
3. Blow air into the bag.
4. Close the bag all the way.
5. Put the bag in a sunny place. Do not spill the water in the cup.
6. Look at the bag in about 1 hour. Look for water drops inside the bag.

Checkpoint

Draw a picture to show what you saw inside the bag. How did the water get from the cup to the sides of the bag?

How do clouds form?

Look in the sky. Can you see any clouds? Clouds form when water evaporates and condenses. Here is how!

Water vapor in the air moves high in the sky. The air and water vapor in it gets colder. The cold water vapor condenses. It changes to tiny drops of water. These water drops form clouds. Now let's make a cloud!

Make a cloud.

You will need: jar ☕ very warm water

⬤ metal lid 🧊 ice cubes

1. Rinse the jar in very warm water.
2. Put a little warm water into the jar.
3. Place the lid upside down on top of the jar.
4. Put ice cubes onto the lid.
5. Watch what happens inside the jar.

Checkpoint

Tell what you saw in the jar. How does the cloud form?

What makes clouds and rain?

Think about a hot, summer day. White, fluffy clouds are in the sky. Then dark gray clouds form and rain falls. The rain stops. The sun comes out. Puddles dry up. New clouds form. Water moving from clouds to the earth and back to clouds again is called the **water cycle.** Find the sun in the picture of the water cycle.

Clouds form.

Water vapor condenses.

Rain falls.

Water evaporates.

The sun heats water in oceans, lakes, and rivers. The water evaporates into the air. In the sky, water vapor condenses and forms clouds.

How does water get back to the earth? Find where rain is falling. Rain falls when drops of water from clouds fall to the ground.

With your finger follow the path of water through the water cycle. Why will your finger make a circle?

Checkpoint

Draw a picture that shows the water cycle.

What are some kinds of clouds?

Close your eyes and think of a cloud. Did your cloud look like any of these clouds?

In sunny weather, you might see clouds that look like feathers. You might see large, white, fluffy clouds before a storm.

You often see gray, flat clouds in rainy weather. These clouds spread across the sky.

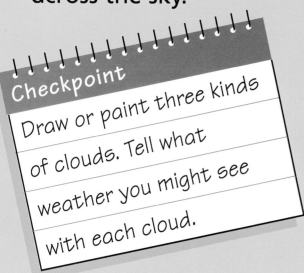

Checkpoint

Draw or paint three kinds of clouds. Tell what weather you might see with each cloud.

These clouds look like feathers.

These white, fluffy clouds look like cotton.

These clouds are gray and flat.

What clouds are highest?

Different clouds are seen in different places in the sky. Some clouds are high in the sky. Other clouds are so low that they seem to touch the tops of tall buildings. Find out where you see different kinds of clouds.

1. Look at the pictures of the clouds. How many kinds of clouds do you see?
2. Draw a chart like this one. Write or draw what each kind of cloud looks like.

where clouds are	what clouds look like
high	
middle	
low	

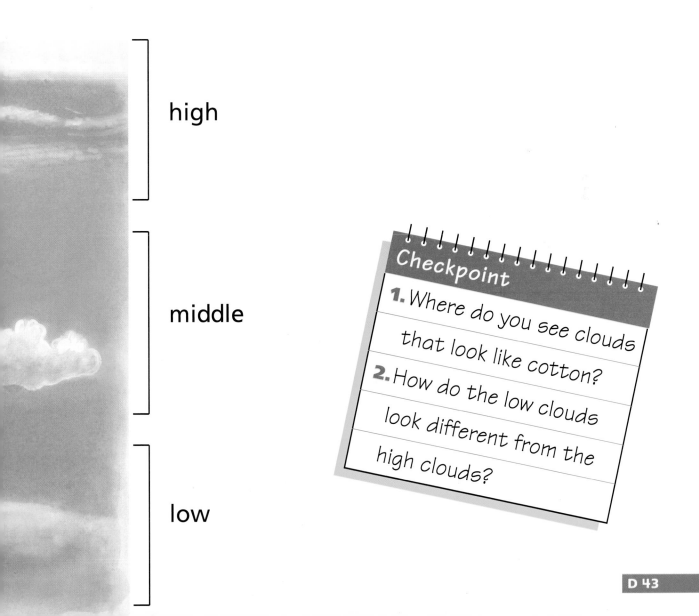

high

middle

Checkpoint
1. Where do you see clouds that look like cotton?
2. How do the low clouds look different from the high clouds?

What did you learn?

You know that water and air are parts of the water cycle. Now show how a puddle of water can be a part of the water cycle.

You will need: crayons   paper   construction paper   pencil

Make a book.

1. Write a story about a puddle of water. Tell how the puddle is part of the water cycle.
2. Draw pictures to go with your story.
3. Use construction paper to make a cover for your book.
4. Put the papers together to make a book.

Puddles

Share what you learned.

1. What happened to your puddle first?
2. How did you end your story?
3. What games can you play with a puddle of water?

Chapter 3

Weather and You

It is raining at the ball game. Do you think these people are wearing clothes for rainy weather?

Knowing about the weather helps people decide what to wear. What did you decide to wear today? Maybe you found out about the weather first!

What do you wear in different weather?

1 Fold a paper into two parts.

2 Write a word to describe one kind of weather at the top of one part. Write a word about different weather at the top of the other part.

3 Draw what you might wear in each kind of weather.

4 **Tell about it.** Tell what you wear in different weather.

Ask me what else I want to find out about what you wear in different weather.

What can you do in different weather?

You can have fun outside in warm sunny weather. But you may get very hot. You may also get a sunburn. How can you stay cool and safe? Maybe you can find a shady place to play. Look at the picture. It shows how you can have fun in sunny weather.

You can also have fun outside in cold, snowy weather. But you need to wear clothes that will keep you warm. What clothes are these children wearing to play in the snow?

Now think about rainy weather. How can you stay dry? You can wear a raincoat and boots. You might carry an umbrella. What else could you do?

Checkpoint

List things you do in different kinds of weather.

How does a coat keep you warm?

When the weather is cold, you wear a coat. How does a coat keep you warm? Try this activity to find out.

You will need:

2 empty cans

warm water

woolen cloth

2 thermometers

masking tape

Find out about it.

1 Wrap the cloth around one can. Use tape to hold the cloth in place.

2 Fill each can with warm water.

3 Put a thermometer in each can.

4 Measure the temperature of the water in each can. Do this every 5 minutes for 20 minutes.

Write about it.

Make a chart like this one. Write down the temperature of the water in each can.

time	temperature of can with cloth	temperature of can without cloth
at start		
after 5 minutes		
after 10 minutes		
after 15 minutes		
after 20 minutes		

Checkpoint

1. Which can of water stayed warmer?

2. Take Action! Tell how a cloth around a can is like a coat you wear on a cold day?

What colors help you stay warm or cool?

What color is your blouse or shirt? Maybe the color can help you stay warm or cool! Some colors keep you warmer on a cold, sunny day. Other colors keep you cooler on a warm, sunny day. Let's find out what different colors do in the sun.

Find out which color keeps you warmer.

You will need:  white cloth    black cloth

 2 thermometers

1. Read the temperature on 2 thermometers.
2. Put the white cloth over 1 thermometer. Put the black cloth over the other one.
3. Put both covered thermometers in a sunny place.
4. Wait 5 minutes. Read the temperature on each thermometer. Cover the thermometers again. Read the temperatures every 5 minutes for 20 minutes.

Checkpoint

Tell which thermometer had the higher temperature. Which color clothes would you wear on a cold, sunny day?

How does weather change in a year?

What is your favorite time of the year? Maybe you like summer best. Summer is one of four seasons. A **season** is a time of year. What are the other seasons?

The pictures show how weather can change in different seasons. What can you wear in different seasons? What things can you do outside?

Checkpoint

Tell what the season is now. What is the weather like where you live?

Winter

The air can be very cold.

Summer

The air can be very hot.

Spring

The air gets warmer.

Fall

The air gets cooler.

How can you measure snow?

You know that many places have snow in the winter. More snow falls in some places than in others. You can measure how much snow falls.

1. Look at the metric ruler in each picture. How much snow fell in each city?

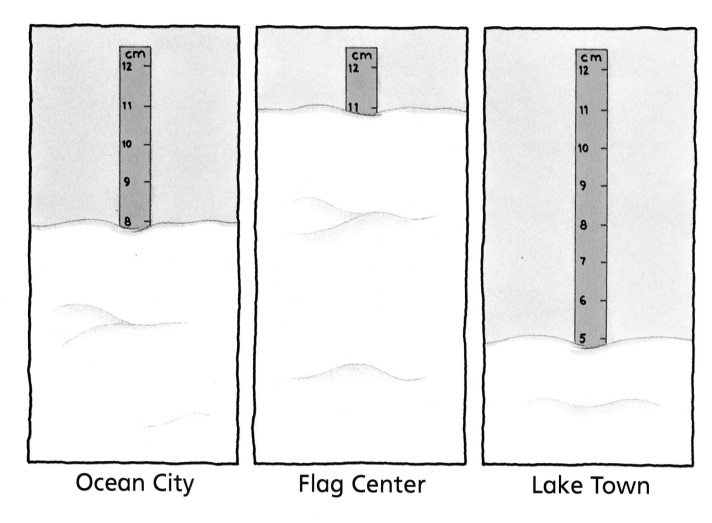

Ocean City   Flag Center   Lake Town

2. Draw a map like this one.

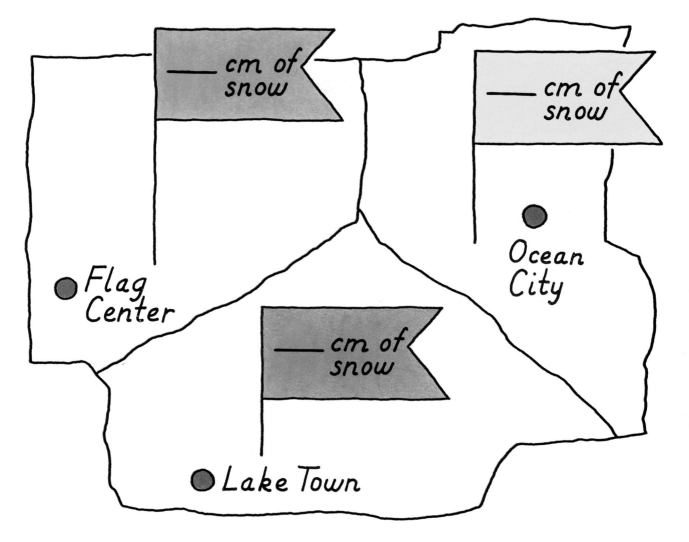

3. Find the name of each city on the map. Write how much snow fell in each city.

What did you learn?

You know what to wear in different weather. You also know what you can do. Now pretend you are a weather reporter on television. Your job is to tell people what the weather will be like. Then people can decide what to wear and what to do.

You will need:  paper   pencil   crayons

Give a weather report.

1. Work with a team. Write a weather report. Tell what the weather will be like tomorrow.
2. Tell what the season is.
3. Tell what people might wear tomorrow.
4. Tell what people can do outdoors.
5. Draw pictures to show with the report.
6. Give your weather report to your class.

Share what you learned.

1. Why is the job of a weather reporter important?
2. Would you like to be a weather reporter? Tell why.

A visit to a weather station

A weather station is a place where people study the weather. When you get there, you see weather maps and computers. You might also see a thermometer and a wind vane.

Some people at a weather station forecast the weather. Forecast means to tell what the weather might be like. The workers who forecast weather are **weather forecasters.** They tell what the weather might be the next day. Or they may tell about next week.

How does a wind vane work?

1 The wind turns the top of the wind vane.

2 The arrow points in the direction the wind comes from.

3 The letters tell a direction. N means north and S means south. E means east and W means west.

Checkpoint

Pretend you are planning to go somewhere. Why would you want to know what the weather will be?

Show what you know.

You know about different kinds of weather. You also know how weather is important to you. Now you can have a weather show to use what you know.

Plan your weather show.

1. Pick a weather project to do.
2. What will you do first?
3. How will your project tell others about weather?

Tell weather riddles.

Make up riddles about the weather. Be sure each riddle ends with *What am I?* Tell your riddles to your classmates. See if your classmates can answer your riddles.

Draw a weather mural.

Draw pictures about weather on mural paper. Show different kinds of weather. Draw the water cycle. Show what you wear in different weather. Hang up your mural!

Make a weather station.

Make a weather station with tools that measure the weather. Show how you use a thermometer and a rain gauge. Show how you use a tool to measure wind.

Share what you know.

1. Share your weather project.
2. How did knowing about weather help you do your project?

Contents

Kids Save Trees

Our classroom trash basket was always full of paper. We knew that trees were cut down to make the paper. We wanted to save some trees. So we decided to use less paper.

We learned a way to make new paper from wastepaper. It was fun to make recycled paper. Here is what we did!

First, we tore some wastepaper into small pieces. We poured warm water on the pieces. After a while, the paper got mushy. Then we stirred the mush with cornstarch.

Next, we spread the paper mush on a screen. We put the screen between the pages of a newspaper. Then we pressed the paper mush to make it flat. We let the paper dry. At last we had recycled paper! We used the paper to make birthday cards.

You can do it.

Think of another way to use less paper. Share your idea with your class.

Kids Get Into Trash

Our class was celebrating Earth Day. We did something special to help the earth. We made a recycling center for our school.

First we got some big boxes. The boxes were for trash. Then we collected trash. We went to every classroom. We filled our boxes with lots of trash.

We collected pieces of chalk and crayons. We collected old notebooks, pens, and pencils. Then we thought of ways to recycle the trash.

Here is how we recycled notebooks. We made note cards from the cardboard covers. The cards are fun to use for art projects. Our teacher saved the wire for science class.

You can do it.

Make a recycling center at home. Show your family how to recycle things.

Kids Make Music

Our class has a box of musical instruments. We have tambourines, triangles, and cymbals. We have sandpaper blocks, bells, and rhythm sticks. But we had no drums, guitars, maracas, or flutes. So we decided to make these musical instruments.

We made instruments from boxes, cans, pans, and jars. We used rubber bands, wax paper, and many other things. Then we decorated our instruments.

When we were finished, we shared our instruments. Each of us played our instrument in different ways. Finally our whole class played our instruments together. We had fun playing our favorite songs. We called our band the Big Bang Band.

You can do it.

Make your own musical instrument from things you find at home. Then use your instrument to play a song.

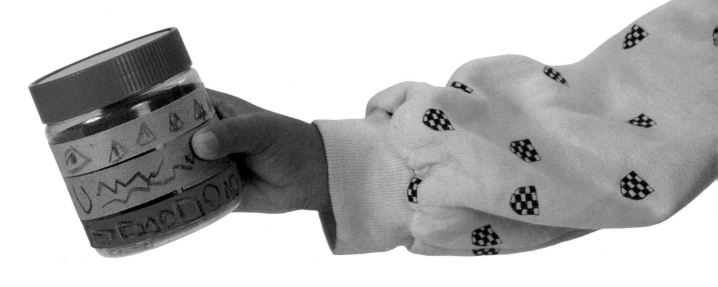

Kids Play Detective

It was a cold, windy day. We could feel cold air inside our school. The air was coming from outside. But where was the cold air coming in? Our class decided to find out.

We got some straws and strips of plastic wrap. Then we made draft detectors. We used our draft detectors to find drafts.

We looked for drafts in all the classrooms. We checked the library and the lunchroom. We held our draft detectors near windows and doors. When the plastic strips moved, we knew that air was coming in.

We made a map of the places where we found drafts. We showed the map to our school custodian.

You can do it.

Make a draft detector. Use it to find drafts in your home. Tell your family where the drafts are.

Places where we found drafts

window

window

Grade I Classroom

door

Study Guide

Answer the questions. Use your own paper.

Chapter 1 Looking at Trees

 1. Look at the pictures. Which picture shows a tree?

a. 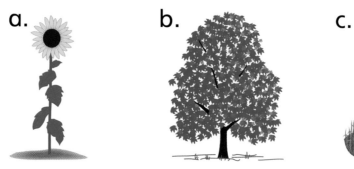 b. c.

2. Trees can be alike or _____ .

thin   tall   different

 3. A _____ grows from the trunk of a tree.

seed   leaf   branch

4. The _____ of most trees grow under the ground.

leaves   roots   trunks

A 10-11 **5.** Trees have different _____ .

water   sun   shapes

A 12-13 **6.** Leaves have different sizes and _____ .

branches   shapes   birds

A 14-15 **7.** Needles fall off of trees _____ of the year.

in the fall   at different times   at the end

A 16-17

A 16-17 **8.** A tree _____ grows into a new tree.

needle   branch   seed

9. Some tree seeds are inside a _____ .

covering   root   leaf

Chapter 2 Looking at Plants

A 22-23 **1.** You can even find plants in _____ .

the air   sidewalk cracks   milk

A 24-25 **2.** A tree trunk is a _____ .

leaf   root   stem

3. Leaves and roots are parts of _____ .

plants   needles   trunks

A 26-27 **4.** Look at the picture. Which plant part makes food for the plant?

a. _____

b. _____

c. _____

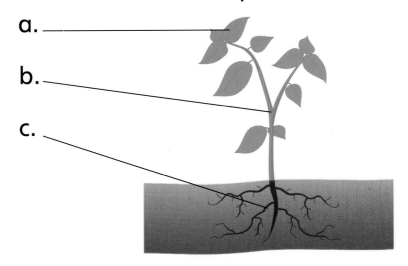

5. A plant cannot live without ____ .

leaves   fruits   wind

A 28-29 **6.** What plant part holds plants in the soil?

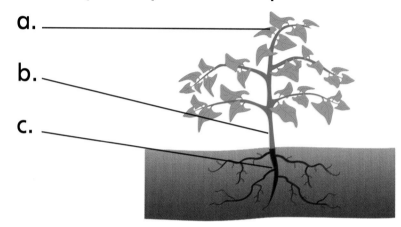

a. _____

b. _____

c. _____

7. Roots take in ____ that the plant needs.

soil   water   wind

A 30-31 **8.** Stems carry water to the ____ .

leaves   soil   tubes

9. Roots and stems have ____ that carry water inside of them.

roots   tubes   soil

A 32-33 **10.** What part of a plant begins to grow from a seed first?

leaves   stem   roots

11. A baby plant and stored food are parts of a ____ .

seed   leaf   soil

A 34-35 **12.** Bean seeds grow best in a ____ place.

cold   warm   pretty

A 36-37 **13.** For plants to grow they need sunlight, air, and ____ .

water   wind   dark

A 38-39 **14.** Different kinds of soil have ____ colors.

the same   dark   different

Chapter 3 How Plants Are Used

A 44-45 **1.** Which comes from plants?

paper clips   apples   crayons

A 46-47 **2.** People use plants for food and ____ .

clothes   sun   glass

A 48-49 **3.** Look at the pictures. Which shows a root that you can eat?

a.   b.   c.

A 50-51 **4.** Many ____ get food from plants.

animals   homes   books

A 52-53 **5.** A ____ can be a home for animals.

seed   tree   pencil

A 54-55 **6.** On a hot day, animals can stay cool in the ____ of a tree.

shade   sunny   seed

Study Guide

Answer the questions. Use your own paper.

Chapter 1 Growing Up

B 4-5 **1.** You _____ as you grow.

look   change   tell

2. You have _____ since you were a baby.

grown   not changed   become smaller

B 6-7 **3.** You can _____ in only one year.

smile   change   play

B 8-9 **4.** Permanent teeth are _____ than first teeth.

whiter   smaller   larger

B 10-11 **5.** Your size and shape change as you _____ .

grow   play   read

6. Look at the pictures. Which picture shows an adult?

a.   b.   c.

B 12-13 **7.** You can get rid of some germs by _____ .

eating   washing   running

8. You need to exercise, rest, eat good food, and keep clean so you can _____ .

be healthy   get sick   not grow

B 14-15 **9.** To stay healthy, you should eat more vegetables than _____ .
bread   fruit   fat

10. You should eat more _____ than meat.
a.   b.   c.

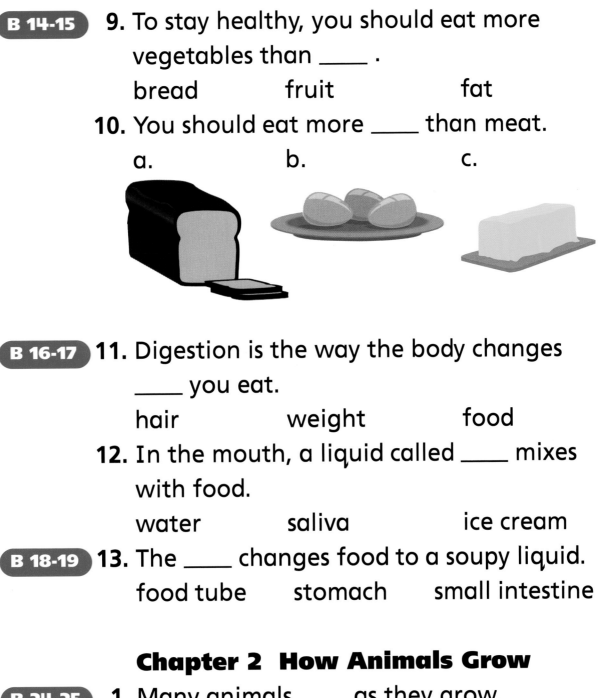

B 16-17 **11.** Digestion is the way the body changes _____ you eat.
hair   weight   food

12. In the mouth, a liquid called _____ mixes with food.
water   saliva   ice cream

B 18-19 **13.** The _____ changes food to a soupy liquid.
food tube   stomach   small intestine

Chapter 2 How Animals Grow

B 24-25 **1.** Many animals _____ as they grow.
make   use   change

Study Guide

B 26-27 **2.** Food, water, a place to live, and _____ are four things animals need to grow.

toys air paper

B 28-29 **3.** A mealworm is a _____ .

larva beetle pupa

4. Animals called _____ hatch from eggs.

rabbits dogs insects

B 30-31 **5.** Mealworms can change in size and _____ .

use shape temperature

B 32-33 **6.** Look at the pictures. Which picture shows a butterfly as it looks when it hatches?

a.

c.

b.

7. A caterpillar changes into a _____ .

pupa covering beetle

B 34-35 **8.** Which of these animals hatch from eggs?

cats birds horses

9. A baby frog is called a _____ .

larva caterpillar tadpole

B 36-37 **10.** Cats and dogs grow inside ____ before they are born.

their mothers   eggs   houses

Chapter 3 Changing Things

B 42-43 **1.** Things change when you ____ them.

use   desk   tree

B 44-45 **2.** You change water when you ____ .

eat   wash   sleep

B 46-47 **3.** What can take dirt out of water?

a filter   some soap   more water

B 48-49 **4.** You change ____ by throwing away trash.

the sky   space   land

B 50-51 **5.** If you ____ things, less trash will go to landfills.

reuse   throw away   waste

B 52-53 **6.** Recycled things are changed and ____ .

thrown away   dirtied   used again

B 54-55 **7.** Look at the pictures. Which one shows things that would make good compost?

a.   b.   c.

Answer the questions. Use your own paper.

Chapter 1 Hearing and Seeing

C 4-5 1. Sounds may be alike or ____ .
different   colorful   hard

C 6-7 2. Sounds can be loud or soft, high or ____ .
low   dark   blue

C 8-9 3. If you pluck a rubber band hard, the rubber band makes a ____ sound.
soft   light   loud

C 10-11 4. Sounds that are ____ can hurt your ears.
soft   low   loud

C 12-13 5. Look at the picture. Which part of the ear is the eardrum?

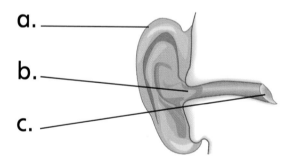

a. ____

b. ____

c. ____

6. You hear sounds when sound messages reach the ____ .
brain   path   outer ear

C 14-15 7. It is easier to tell where sounds come from with ____ .
two ears   your eyes   one ear

C 16-17 **8.** You need ____ to see.

a nose   darkness   light

C 18-19 **9.** Look at the picture. Which part of the eye is the pupil?

a.

b.

c.

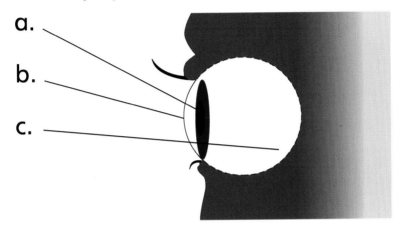

C 20-21 **10.** It is easier to catch a ball when you ____ .

use two eyes   close your eyes   use one eye

Chapter 2   Making Sounds

C 26-27 **1.** When you pluck a rubber band to make a sound, the rubber band ____ .

moves back and forth   stays still   breaks

C 28-29 **2.** When objects move back and forth quickly, they ____ .

break   vibrate   bend

3. When objects vibrate, they make ____ .

rubber bands   smiles   sounds

C 30-31 **4.** Sound can ____ through objects.

travel   play   see

5. Sound can be heard best when it travels through _____ .

wood water air

C 32-33 **6.** Sound travels through the air _____ .

only up in all directions only down

7. You hear sound through air because sound makes air _____ .

vibrate stop warm

C 34-35 **8.** A string telephone shows you that sound travels _____ .

lightly through a string slowly

C 36-37 **9.** The _____ of your ear is good for catching sounds.

size and shape color trumpet

C 38-39 **10.** The sounds of different instruments _____ to make music.

shine come together march

11. Look at the picture. Which part of the drum vibrates the most when you play it?

a.

b.

c.

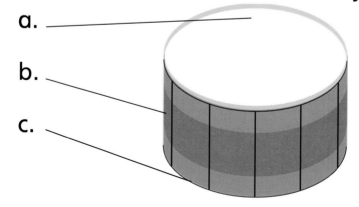

Chapter 3 Light

C 44-45 **1.** Light travels in a _____ .
straight line   wavy line   circle

C 46-47 **2.** Light _____ move through a wall.
can   can not   always will

3. Light is stopped by _____ .
plastic wrap   wood   air

C 48-49 **4.** When light _____ through an object, a shadow forms.
can not go   travels   moves

C 50-51 **5.** Light bounces best when it hits _____ objects.
rough, dark   smooth, shiny   smooth, dark

C 52-53 **6.** Look at the pictures. Which one shows that water can make objects look different?

a.    b.    c.

C 54-55 **7.** Light is made up of _____ .
one color   no color   many colors

Answer the questions. Use your own paper.

Chapter 1 Describing Weather

D 4-5 **1.** Which word tells about weather?

cloudy   travel   hard

D 6-7 **2.** Weather can ____ during the day.

chart   stop   change

D 8-9 **3.** The ____ tells how warm the air is.

tube   temperature   wind

4. You can find the temperature of air by using a ____ .

flag   rain gauge   thermometer

5. As air gets warmer, the liquid inside a thermometer moves ____ .

down   sideways   up

D 10-11 **6.** Another name for moving air is ____ .

temperature   wind   flag

D 12-13 **7.** Look at the pictures. In which picture is the wind blowing hardest?

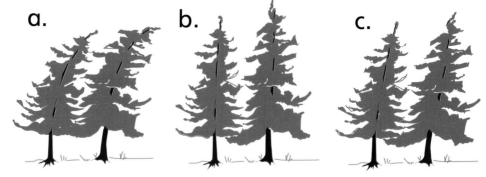
a.   b.   c.

D 14-15 **8.** A tool you can use to measure rainfall is called a ____ .

rain gauge rain cap thermometer

D 16-17 **9.** During a thunderstorm you usually see dark clouds, rain, and ____ .

snow   lightning   sunshine

Chapter 2 Air, Water, and Weather

D 22-23 **1.** You cannot see ____ , but it is all around.

rain   sun   air

D 24-25 **2.** Look at the pictures. Which picture shows that there is water in the air?

a.   b.   c.

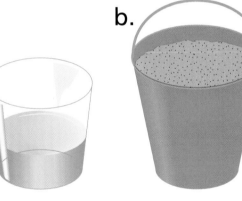

D 26-27 **3.** Water that is in the air is called ____ .

water vapor cool water wet water

4. When water vapor ____ , it changes to liquid water.

evaporates heats condenses

D 28-29 **5.** Puddles dry up after all the water ____ .

evaporates condenses gets cold

6. When liquid water evaporates, it changes to _____ .

rain water vapor a puddle

D 30-31 **7.** Puddles will dry quickly on a _____ day.

rainy cold windy

D 32-33 **8.** Water evaporates faster in the _____ .

shade sun winter

D 34-35 **9.** When water vapor moves high in the sky, it cools and _____ .

condenses evaporates forms a puddle

D 36-37 **10.** Look at the pictures. What forms when water vapor condenses?

a. b. c.

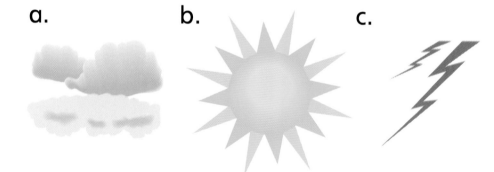

D 38-39 **11.** Water moves from clouds to the earth and back to clouds again in the _____ .

rain water cycle storm

D 40-41 **12.** When do you see clouds that look like feathers?

in a storm on rainy days on sunny days

Chapter 3 Weather and You

D 46-47 1. Knowing about weather helps you choose
what to ____ .
wear   say   eat

D 48-49 2. When the weather is ____ , you might
play in the shade.
cold and snowy   sunny and hot   rainy

3. Look at the picture. What kind of weather
is this child dressed for?
cold and snowy   warm and sunny   rainy

D 50-51 4. In cold weather, a coat keeps you ____ .
cold   wet   warm

D 52-53 5. Wear ____ colors to stay warm on a cold,
sunny day.
light   dark   pretty

6. To stay cool, what is the best color to
wear on a hot, sunny day?
yellow   black   white

D 54-55 7. A ____ is a time of year.
clock   season   weather

Scientists like to learn about the world. They like to help with problems. They use scientific methods to find answers. Scientists use many steps in their methods. Sometimes they use the steps in different ways. You can use these steps to do experiments.

Explain the Problem

Ask a question like this. Does sound travel?

Make Observations

Tell about the size, color, or shape
of things.

Give a Hypothesis

Try to answer the problem. Tell your idea.
Then do the experiment.

Make a Chart or Graph

Tell what you saw in your chart or graph.

Make Conclusions

Decide if your hypothesis is right or wrong.

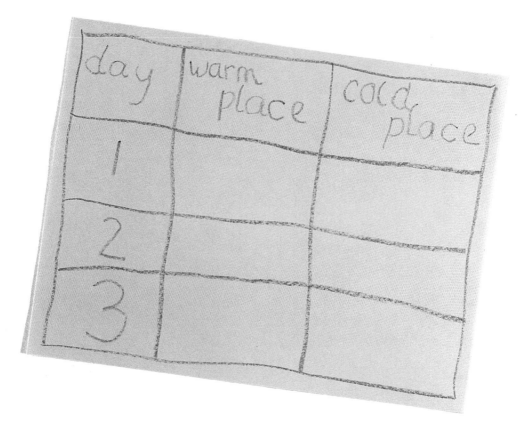

Safety in Science

Scientists are careful when they do experiments. You need to be careful too. Here are some rules to remember.

- Read each experiment carefully.

- Wear cover goggles when needed.

- Clean up spills right away.

- Never taste or smell unknown things.

- Do not shine lights in someone's eyes.

- Put things away when you are done.

- Wash your hands after each experiment.

Experiment with Plants and Light

Brad is watering his plants. One plant is bent. It is leaning toward the window. Brad thinks the plant is bending toward light. He wonders if other plants bend toward light.

Problem

Do some plants bend toward light?

Give Your Hypothesis

Answer the problem.
Then do the experiment.

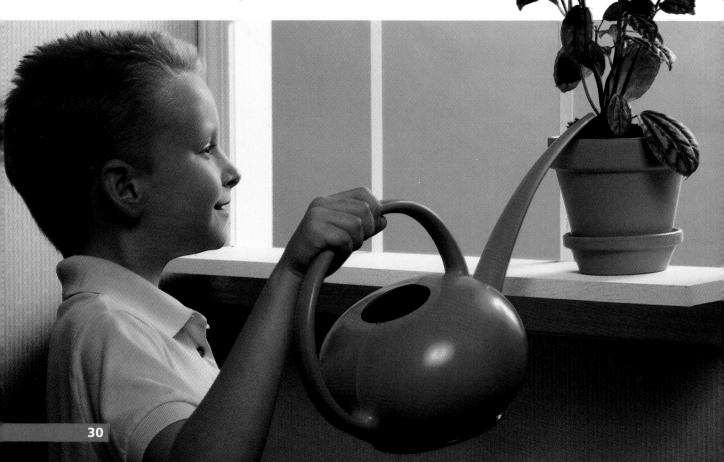

Follow the Directions

1 Make a chart like this one.

time	bends toward light
after 1 week	
1 week after turning plant	

2 Put a small plant near a sunny window for one week.

3 Does the plant bend toward light? Write yes or no in your chart.

4 Turn the plant so it bends away from the window. Leave it for 1 week.

5 Write in your chart if the plant bends.

Tell Your Conclusion

Do some plants bend toward light?

Experiment with Brushing

Jack rinses his mouth after lunch. This makes his mouth feel clean. He wonders why he needs to brush. Can just water clean his teeth? Jack wonders if brushing cleans better than just rinsing.

Problem

Does brushing help make things clean?

Give Your Hypothesis

Answer the problem.
Then do the experiment.

Follow the Directions

1 Make a chart like this one.

how I cleaned spoon	Is spoon clean?
rinsing	
brushing	

2 Rub peanut butter on 2 spoons. Let the spoons sit for 2 hours.

3 Run water over 1 spoon. Does rinsing help clean the spoon?

4 Scrub the other spoon with a brush.

5 Does brushing help clean the spoon? Write your answers in your chart.

6 Circle in the chart which way cleans better.

Tell Your Conclusion

Does brushing help make things clean?

Experiment with Color

Debra just became a crossing guard. She brought home her orange belt. Her brother Matt thinks orange is ugly. He likes blue.

Matt wonders why the belts are orange or yellow. He notices that the school bus also is yellow. He wonders if yellow is easy to see.

Problem

Is it easier to see yellow than blue?

Give Your Hypothesis

Answer the problem.
Then do the experiment.

Follow the Directions

1 Make a chart like this one.

color	easy to see
yellow	
blue	

2 Get a piece of bright yellow paper.
Tape it against a gray paper.
Can you see the yellow easily?
Write the answer in your chart.

3 Then get a piece of blue paper. Tape it against the gray paper. Can you see the blue easily? Fill in your chart.

4 Which color is easier to see? Circle the color in your chart.

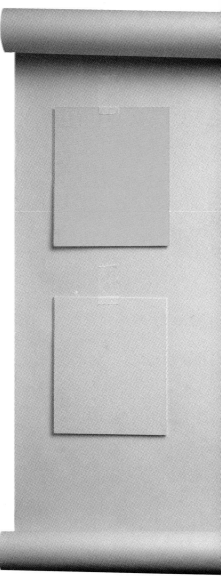

Tell Your Conclusion

Is it easier to see yellow than blue?

Experiment with a Thermometer

Kim and Mary are walking home from school. They take off their coats. They needed their coats this morning. It was cool then. Now it is warm. Kim and Mary think the air gets warmer during the day.

Problem

Can air get warmer during the day?

Give Your Hypothesis

Answer the problem.
Then do the experiment.

Follow the Directions

1 Make a chart like this one.

time	temperature
morning	
afternoon	

2 Put a thermometer outside.

3 Read the temperature in the morning.

4 Read the temperature in the afternoon.

5 Read the temperature in the morning and afternoon for 2 days.

6 When is the temperature highest? When is it lowest? Write your answers in your chart. Circle which time of day is warmer.

Tell Your Conclusion

Can air get warmer during the day?

A **adult,** p. B10, An adult is a living thing that is full grown.

B **baby plant,** p. A30, A baby plant is on the inside of a seed. Baby plants can grow into adult plants.

bark, p. A52, Bark covers the trunk and branches of trees.

beetle, p. B28, A beetle is an insect with two shiny front wings. The front wings cover the two back wings when the beetle is not flying.

brain, p. C12, The brain is a part of the body that is inside the head. The brain helps people think, feel, move, see, and hear.

branch, p. A6, A branch is the part of a tree that grows out from the trunk.

broad leaf, p. A14, A broad leaf is a leaf that is flat.

butterfly, p. B32, A butterfly is an insect. Butterflies have four wings that have bright colors.

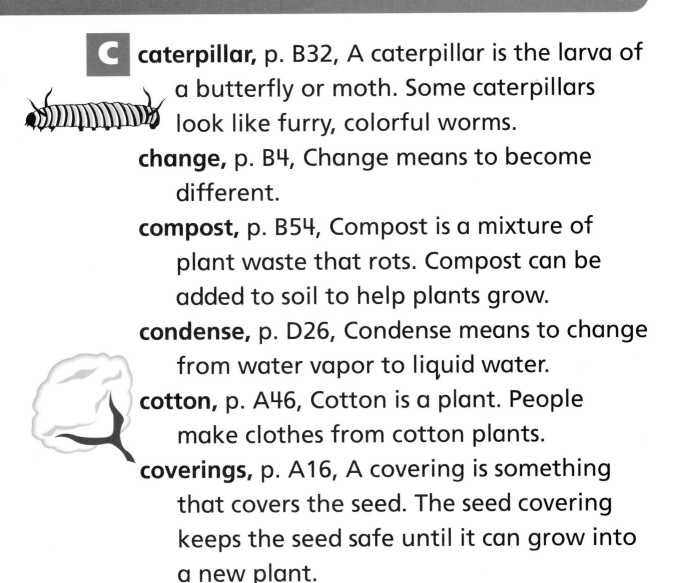

C **caterpillar,** p. B32, A caterpillar is the larva of a butterfly or moth. Some caterpillars look like furry, colorful worms.

change, p. B4, Change means to become different.

compost, p. B54, Compost is a mixture of plant waste that rots. Compost can be added to soil to help plants grow.

condense, p. D26, Condense means to change from water vapor to liquid water.

cotton, p. A46, Cotton is a plant. People make clothes from cotton plants.

coverings, p. A16, A covering is something that covers the seed. The seed covering keeps the seed safe until it can grow into a new plant.

D **digestion,** p. B16, Digestion changes food so that the body can use it.

E **eardrum,** p. C12, The eardrum is the skin at the end of the tunnel in the ear. The eardrum moves when sound hits it.

evaporate, p. D28, Evaporate means to change from liquid water to water vapor.

exercise, p. B12, Exercise is moving your body to stay healthy. Running, swimming, and playing ball are kinds of exercise.

 filter, p. B46, A filter is used to take dirt out of water, other liquids, or air.

first teeth, p. B8, First teeth are the teeth people get when they are babies.

flower, p. A25, A flower is the part of a plant that makes seeds.

food tube, p. B18, The food tube is a part of the body. Food goes from the mouth to the stomach through the food tube.

 germ, p. B13, A germ is very tiny and can be seen only with a microscope. Germs can make you sick.

group, p. A12, A group is a set of objects that are alike in some way.

H **hatch,** p. B28, Hatch means to come out of an egg.

healthy, p. B12, Healthy means to be well, or not sick.

I

inner ear parts, p. C12, Inner ear parts are the parts that are inside the head. The inner ear parts send sound messages to the brain.

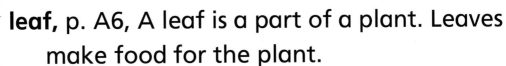

insect, p. B28, An insect is a very small animal. Insects have three body parts and six legs.

instrument, p. C38, An instrument is something that makes music.

L

landfill, p. B48, A landfill is a large place where trash is buried.

larva, p. B28, A larva is the insect form that hatches from an egg. The larva often looks like a worm.

leaf, p. A6, A leaf is a part of a plant. Leaves make food for the plant.

lens, p. C19, The lens is the clear part of the eye. The lens is behind the pupil.

light, p. C42, Light comes from the sun, flashlights, and other things.

lumber, p. A56, Lumber is wood that is cut into boards.

 mealworm, p. B25, A mealworm is the larva of a beetle.

 **needle,** p. A14, A needle is a leaf that is thin and pointed.

noise, p. C10, Noise is sound that you do not like to hear. Loud noises can sometimes hurt your ears.

permanent teeth, p. B8, Permanent teeth are the new teeth that grow in when a person's first teeth fall out.

plant, p. A22, A plant is a living thing. Most plants can make their own food from sunlight, air, and water.

pupa, p. B28, A pupa is the form of an insect that the larva changes into. The pupa changes into an adult.

pupil, p. C19, The pupil is the opening in the center of the eye. Light enters the eye through the pupil.

R **rain gauge,** p. D14, A rain gauge is used to measure how much rain falls.

rainfall, p. D14, Rainfall is how much rain, snow, or sleet fall.

recycle, p. B52, Recycle means to change something so that it can be used again.

rest, p. B12, Rest is being still or quiet, or sleeping.

reuse, p. B50, Reuse means to use something, such as a lunch bag, again.

root, p. A7, A root is a part of a plant. Roots hold plants in the ground.

rot, p. B54, Rot means to break down or to become spoiled.

S **saliva,** p. B16, Saliva is a liquid in the mouth. Saliva helps to digest food.

season, p. D54, A season is one of the four parts of the year. The seasons are spring, summer, fall, and winter.

seed, p. A16, A seed is the part of a plant that grows into a new plant. Seeds are made in flowers.

seed coat, p. A30, A seed coat is the outside part of a seed.

shade, p. A54, Shade is a place that is not in bright sunlight. Shady places are cooler than sunny places.

shadow, p. C48, A shadow is a dark shape that is made when an object blocks light.

small intestine, p. B18, The small intestine is a long, winding tube in the body. The small intestine changes food so that the body can use it.

soil, p. A38, Soil is the top layer of the earth. Plants grow in soil.

sort, p. A12, Sort means to put together things that are alike.

sound, p. C4, A sound is something you hear. A sound is made when an object vibrates.

stem, p. A24, A stem is the main part of a plant. Stems hold plants up and carry water and food to other plant parts.

stomach, p. B18, The stomach is a part of the body. The stomach changes food into a soupy liquid.

stored food, p. A30, Stored food is inside a seed. The baby plant uses the stored food to start growing.

T **tadpole,** p. B35, A tadpole is a very young frog or toad. Tadpoles have tails and live only in water.

temperature, p. D8, Temperature is a measurement of how hot or cold something is.

thermometer, p. D8, A thermometer is used to measure temperature.

thunderstorm, p. D16, A thunderstorm is a kind of weather that has strong winds, heavy rain, lightning, and thunder.

tree, p. A4, A tree is a large plant with a trunk, branches, and leaves.

trunk, p. A6, A trunk is the stem of a tree.

tube, p. A28, The tubes in plant roots and stems carry water or food.

tunnel, p. C13, A tunnel leads from the outside of the ear to the eardrum. Sounds move through the tunnel.

vibrate, p. C28, Vibrate means to move back and forth very quickly.

 waste, p. B54, Waste is something that has been thrown away.

water cycle, p. D38, The water cycle is the movement of water between the air and the earth.

water vapor, p. D26, Water vapor is a form of water in the air. When liquid water evaporates, it changes to water vapor.

weather, p. D4, Weather is what the air outside is like. The air may be still or windy, hot or cold, wet or dry.

wind, p. D10, Wind is moving air.

wood, p. A47, Wood is the hard part of the trunk and branches of a tree.

Acknowledgments

Outside Credits
Interior Design
Kym Abrams Design, Inc.
The Quarasan Group, Inc.
Rosa + Wesley Design Associates

Unless otherwise acknowledged, all photographs are the property of Scott, Foresman and Company. Page abbreviations are as follows: **(T) top, (C) center, (B) bottom, (L) left, (R) right, (INS) inset.**

Module A
Photographs
Front & Back Cover: Background: John Shaw/Bruce Coleman, Inc.   Children's Photos: Michael Goss for Scott, Foresman and Company.

Page A4(L) Zig Leszczynski/EARTH SCENES
A4-A5 John Eastcott/YVA Momatiuk/The Image Works
A5(L) E.R.Degginger   **A5(R)** Susan McCartney/
Photo Researchers, Inc.   **A8(T)** R.F.Head/EARTH SCENES
A8(B) Grant Heilman Photography   **A9(TL)** E.R.Degginger
A9(TR) William E.Ferguson   **A9(B)** John Shaw/
Bruce Coleman, Inc.   **A10(L&R)** John Shaw/Bruce Coleman, Inc.
A10(C) E.R.Degginger   **A30** Willard Clay Photography
A46 Jean-Claude Carton/Bruce Coleman, Inc.
A54 H.Confer/The Image Works   **A60** Mark Burnett/Stock Boston

Illustrations
Page A2 Jan Palmer   **A6-7** Lois Leonard Stock
A18-19 Jan Palmer   **A22-23** Diana Philbrook
A24-25 Erika Kors   **A28** Ebet Dudley   **A32** Erika Kors
A36-37 Ilene Robinette   **A40-41** Linda Hawkins
A52-53 Cindy Brodie   **A55** Jan Palmer   **A61** Mike Eagle

Module B
Photographs
Front & Back Cover: Background: E.R.Degginger   Children's Photos: Michael Goss for Scott, Foresman and Company.

Page B2 Ron Rovtar/FPG   **B3** John Shaw/Tom Stack & Associates
B4-B5 Luann Benoit   **B6(T)** Ron Rovtar/FPG   **B13(T)** Brent Jones/
Tony Stone Worldwide   **B24(L)** Larry Lefever/Grant Heilman
Photography   **B24(R)** Thomas Howland/Grant Heilman
Photography   **B24(T)** Barry L.Runk/Grant Heilman Photography
B25(B) Sonia Wasco/Grant Heilman Photography
B26-B27 Stephen J.Krasemann/DRK Photo
B32(L&R) & B33 John Shaw/Tom Stack & Associates
B34 E.R.Degginger   **B48** Willie L.Hill

Illustrations
Page B9 Ka Botzis   **B14** Deborah Morse   **B18** Deborah Morse
B20 Deborah Morse   **B28-29** Laurie O'Keefe   **B35** Lois Leonard
Stock   **B36-37** Edward Brooks   **B38-39** Lois Leonard Stock
B42-43 Andrea Z. Tachiera   **B44-45** Susan Spellman
B56-57 Nancy Lee Walter   **B61** Mike Eagle

Module C
Photographs
Front & Back Cover: Background: Gary A.Conner/PhotoEdit
Children's Photos: Michael Goss for Scott, Foresman and Company.

Page C2 L.L.T.Rhodes/ EARTH SCENES   **C3** E.R.Degginger
C6 Thomas Wanstall/The Image Works   **C7(L)** John Cancalosi/
Peter Arnold, Inc.   **C7(R)** Don & Pat Valenti   **C10** L.L.T.Rhodes/
EARTH SCENES   **C36** The Bettmann Archive
C52(B) E.R.Degginger   **C53(T)** CoCo McCoy/Rainbow
C54 Runk/Schoenberger/Grant Heilman Photography
C55 E.R.Degginger

Illustrations
Page C4-5 Meryl Henderson   **C12-13** Precision Graphics
C18-19 Deborah Morse   **C22-23** Ebet Dudley
C26-27 Roberta Polfus   **C32-33** Ilene Robinette
C40 Lisa Pompelli   **C61** Mike Eagle

Module D
Photographs
Front & Back Cover: Background: Tom Bean/DRK Photo
Children's Photos: Michael Goss for Scott, Foresman and Company.

Page D2 Jeff Persons/Stock Boston   **D6** Jerry Howard/Stock
Boston   **D10** Tony Arruza/Bruce Coleman, Inc.
D16(L) Bruce Davidson/EARTH SCENES
D16(R) Barry Parker/Bruce Coleman, Inc.   **D17(L)**
R.F.Myers/Visuals Unlimited   **D17(R)** S.Savino/The Image Works
D22-D23 Joseph A.DiChello   **D27** Garv Griffen/ANIMALS
ANIMALS   **D36** James Tallon   **D39** Stephen J.Krasemann/DRK
Photo   **D40-D41** David R.Frazier   **D41(T)** Tom Bean/DRK Photo
D41(B) Charlton Photographs   **D46-47** Ben Simmons/Stock
Market   **D48** Bob Daemmrich/Tony Stone Worldwide
D49 Jeff Persons/Stock Boston   **D60** Brownie Harris/The Stock
Market

Illustrations
Page D2 Linda Hawkins   **D3** Susan Spellman
D4-5 Andrea Z. Tachiera   **D8** Linda Hawkins   **D12-13** Ted Carr
D18 Judy Sakaguchi   **D28** Susan Spellman
D32-33 Rondi Collette   **D42-43** Sharron O'Neil
D54-55 Jan Palmer   **D56-57** Nancy Lee Walter
D61 Mike Eagle

Back Matter
Illustrations
Pages 10-25, 38-46 Precision Graphics